HEART ON THE LEFT

Books available by Adrian Mitchell

POETRY

Love Songs of World War Three (Allison & Busby/W.H. Allen, 1989)
Greatest Hits: His 40 Golden Greats (Bloodaxe Books, 1991)
Blue Coffee: Poems 1985-1996 (Bloodaxe Books, 1996)
Heart on the Left: Poems 1953-1984 (Bloodaxe Books, 1997)

PLAYS

The Pied Piper (Oberon Books)
Gogol: The Government Inspector (Methuen)
Calderón: The Mayor of Zalamea & two other plays (Absolute Classics)
Lope de Vega: Fuente Ovejuna and Lost in a Mirror (Absolute Classics)
Tyger Two, Man Friday, Satie Day/Night and *In the Unlikely Event of an Emergency* (Oberon Books)
The Siege (Oberon Books)

POETRY FOR CHILDREN

The Orchard Book of Poems (Orchard, 1993)
The Thirteen Secrets of Poetry (Macdonald, 1993)
Balloon Lagoon (Orchard, 1997)

CHILDREN'S STORIES

Our Mammoth
Our Mammoth Goes to School
Our Mammoth in the Snow
The Baron Rides Out
The Baron on the Island of Cheese
The Baron All at Sea
    (all Walker Books)
The Ugly Duckling (Dorling Kindersley)
The Steadfast Tin Soldier (Dorling Kindersley)
Maudie and the Green Children (Tradewind)
Gynormous! The Ultimate Book of Giants (Orion)

Heart on the LEFT

POEMS

1953-1984

Adrian MITCHELL

with pictures by Ralph STEADman

BLOODAXE BOOKS

Poems copyright © Adrian Mitchell 1997
Pictures copyright © Ralph Steadman 1997

ISBN: 1 85224 414 3

First published 1997 by
Bloodaxe Books Ltd,
P.O. Box 1SN,
Newcastle upon Tyne NE99 1SN.

Bloodaxe Books Ltd acknowledges
the financial assistance of Northern Arts.

Cover printing by J. Thomson Colour Printers Ltd, Glasgow.

Printed in Great Britain by
Cromwell Press Ltd, Broughton Gifford, Melksham, Wiltshire.

For my wife, Celia.
For my children, Alistair, Danny, Briony, Sasha, Boty and Beattie.
For my grandchildren.
For all those who work for peace and justice.

ACKNOWLEDGEMENTS

Heart on the Left contains nearly all my published poems up to 1985, when my book *Blue Coffee* takes over. Most of the poems from previous books – *Poems, Out Loud, Ride the Nightmare* and *The Apeman Cometh* (all published by Jonathan Cape) and *On the Beach at Cambridge* (Allison & Busby) – will be found here. I've also added a few favourite lyrics from my plays and operas, some of them from my book *Love Songs of World War Three* (Allison & Busby).

EDUCATION HEALTH WARNING

None of the work in this or any other of my books is to be used in connection with any examination whatsoever. Reduce the size of classes in State schools to twelve and I might reconsider.

CONTENTS

MY NATIVE ARCHIPELAGO

RELIGION, ROYALTY AND THE ARTS

LOVE, THE APEMAN, CURSES, BLESSINGS AND FRIENDS

THE COLLECTED WORKS OF APEMAN MUDGEON

SONGS FROM SOME OF THE SHOWS

OUR BLUE PLANET

My Native Archipelago

To You

One: we were swaddled, ugly-beautiful and drunk on milk.
Two: cuddled in arms always covered by laundered sleeves.
Three: we got sand and water to exercise our imaginative faculties.
Four: we were hit. Suddenly hit.

Five: we were fed to the educational system limited.
Six: worried by the strange creatures in our heads, we strangled some of them.
Seven: we graduated in shame.
Eight: World War Two and we hated the Germans as much as our secret
    bodies, loved the Americans as much as the Russians, hated killing, loved
    killing, depending on the language in the Bible in the breast pocket of
    the dead soldier, we were crazy-thirsty for Winston Superman, for Jesus
    with his infinite tommy-gun and the holy Spitfires, while the Japanese
    hacked through the undergrowth of our nightmares – there were pits full
    of people-meat – and the real bombs came, but they didn't hit us, my
    love, they didn't hit us exactly.
My love, they are trying to drive us mad.

So we got to numbers eight, nine, ten, and eleven,
Growing scales over every part of our bodies,
Especially our eyes,
Because scales were being worn, because scales were armour.
And now we stand, past thirty, together, madder than ever,
We make a few diamonds and lose them.
We sell our crap by the ton.
My love, they are trying to drive us mad.

Make love. We must make love
Instead of making money.
You know about rejection? Hit. Suddenly hit.
Want to spend my life building poems in which untamed
People and animals walk around freely, lie down freely
Make love freely
In the deep loving carpets, stars circulating in their ceilings,
Poems like honeymoon planetariums.
But our time is burning.
My love, they are trying to drive us mad.

Peace was all I ever wanted.
It was too expensive.
My love, they are trying to drive us mad.

Half the people I love are sh rinking.
My love, they are trying to drive us mad.

Half the people I love are exploding.
My love, they are trying to drive us mad.

I am afraid of going mad.

Icarus Schmicarus

If you never spend your money
you know you'll always have some cash.
If you stay cool and never burn
you'll never turn to ash.
If you lick the boots that kick you
then you'll never feel the lash
and if you crawl along the ground
at least you'll never crash.
So why why why –
WHAT MADE YOU THINK YOU COULD FLY?

C'mon Everybody

There's a grand old dance that's rockin the nation
Shake your money and shut your mouth
Taking the place of copulation
S'called The Bourgeois.

See that girl with the diamond thing?
Shake your money and shut your mouth
Didn't get that by picketing
She done The Bourgeois.

Do-gooder, do-gooder where you been?
Shake your money and shut your mouth
Done myself good, got a medal from the Queen
For The Bourgeois.

  Is it a singer? No.
  Is it a lover? No.
  Is it a bourgeois? Yeaaah!

Wave your missile around the vault
Shake your money and shut your mouth
Somebody suffers well it ain't your fault
That you're Bourgeois.

I play golf so I exist
Shake your money and shut your mouth
Eye on the ball and hand over fist
I do The Bourgeois.

Five days a week on the nine-eleven
Shake your money and shut your mouth
When we die we'll go to Bournemouth
Cos we're Bourgeois.

To Nye Bevan Despite His Change of Heart

Because I loved him
I believe that somebody dropped blood-freezing powder
Into the water-jug of vodka Nye Bevan swigged
Before he asked us:
Do you want Britain to go naked to the conference table?

A difficult question.
Whoever saw Britain naked?
Britain bathes behind locked doors
Where even the loofah is subject to the Official Secrets Act.
But surely Britain strips for love-making?
Not necessarily.
An analysis of British sexual response
Proves that most of the United Kingdom's acts of love
Have been undertaken unilaterally.
There have been persistently malicious rumours
From Africa and Asia
That Britain's a habitual rapist
But none of the accusers have alleged
That Britain wore anything less than full dress uniform
With a jangle of medals, bash, bash,
During the alleged violations.

So do you want Britain to go naked to the conference table?
Britain the mixed infant,
Its mouth sullen as it enters its second millennium
Of pot-training.
Britain driven mad by puberty,
Still wearing the uniform of Lord Baden-Powell
(Who was honoured for his services to sexual mania).
Britain laying muffins at the Cenotaph.
Britain, my native archipelago
Entirely constructed of rice pudding.

So do you want Britain to go naked to the conference table?
Yes. Yes Nye, without any clothes at all.
For underneath the welded Carnaby
Spike-studded dog-collar groincrusher boots,
Blood-coloured combinations
And the golfing socks which stink of Suez,
Underneath the Rolls Royce heart
Worn on a sleeve encrusted with royal snot,
Underneath the military straitjacket
From the Dead Meat Boutique –
      Lives
      A body
Of incredibly green beauty.

I Tried, I Really Tried

Mesh-faced loudspeakers outshouted Fleet Street,
Their echoes overlapping down Shoe Lane
And Bouverie Street, pronouncing:
WASH YOURSELF POET.
Blurred black police cars from the BBC
Circled me blaring: WASH YOURSELF POET
AND DON'T FORGET YOUR NAVEL.
My ears were clogged with savoury gold wax
And so I failed WASH to hear at first WASH.
WASH WASH YOURSELF
Since I was naked and they wore
Chrome-armoured cars and under the cars man-made fibre suits and under
    the suits Y-front pants and under the pants official groin protectors and
    under the groin protectors automatics,

I obediently ran to the city's pride,
The Thames, that Lord Mayor's Procession of mercury,
And jumped from Westminster Bridge.
Among half-human mud I bathed
Using a dead cat for a loofah,
Detergent foam for gargle.
I dived, heard the power station's rumble and the moan of sewers.
The bubbles of my breath exploded along the waterskin.
Helmeted in dead newspapers, I sprang
Into the petrol-flavoured air
And Big Ben, like a speak-your-weight machine
Intoned WATCH YOURSELF POET.
Clothed in the muck of London, I yelled back:
I HAVE BEEN WASHED IN THE BLOOD OF THE THAMES,
BIG BROTHER, AND FROM NOW ON I SHALL USE NO OTHER.

As I Write There Is a Procession Passing My Window

BANG BANG BANG
TARA CHI-TUM TITA

    I am very old
    I have to get up three times in the morning and sleep after lunch

BANG BANG BANG
TARA CHI-TUM TITA

    I am so old
    I am still paying off my danegeld at a poem a month

VOTE VOTE VOTE FOR MR MANDRAKE
(Scream)
HE'S THE MAN TO SEE YOU THROUGH
BANG BANG

    I am extremely old
    I remember when the coastlines on maps were completely different
    I remember when Mars Bars were as big as sliced loaves.

BANG BANG BANG
TARA CHI-TUM TITA

I am so damned old and tired
With the sex war the class war the race war the war war

BANG BANG BANG

I can remember nothing but war

Nostalgia – Now Threepence Off

Where are they now, the heroes of furry-paged books and comics brighter than
life which packed my ink-lined desk in days when BOP meant *Boys' Own Paper*,
where are they anyway?

Where is Percy F. Westerman? Where are H.L. Gee and Arthur Mee? Why
is Edgar Rice (*The Warlord of Mars*) Burroughs, the *Bumper Fun Book* and the
Wag's Handbook? Where is the *Wonder Book of Reptiles*? Where the hell is *The
Boy's Book of Bacteriological Warfare*?

Where are the *Beacon Readers*? Did Rover, that tireless hound, devour his
mon-o-syll-ab-ic-all-y correct family? Did Little Black Sambo and Epaminondas
shout for Black Power?

Did Peter Rabbit get his when myxomatosis came around the second time,
did the Flopsy Bunnies stiffen to a standstill, grow bug-eyed, fly-covered and
then disintegrate?

Where is G.A. Henty and his historical lads – Wolfgang the Hittite, Armpit
the Young Viking, Cyril who lived in Sodom? Where are their uncorrupted
bodies and Empire-building brains, England needs them, the *Sunday Times*
says so.

There is news from the Strewelpeter mob. Johnny-Head-In-Air spends his
days reporting flying saucers, the telephone receiver never cools from the heat
of his hand. Little Harriet, who played with matches, still burns, but not with
fire. The Scissor-man is everywhere.

Babar the Elephant turned the jungle into a garden city. But things went
wrong. John and Susan, Titty and Roger, became unaccountably afraid of
water, sold their dinghies, all married each other, live in a bombed-out cinema
on surgical spirits and weeds of all kinds.

Snow White was in the *News of the World* – Virgin Lived With Seven Midgets,
Court Told. And in the psychiatric ward an old woman dribbles as she mumbles
about a family of human bears, they ate porridge, yes Miss Goldilocks of course
they did.

Hans Brinker vainly whirled his silver skates round his head as the jackboots
of Emil and the Detectives invaded his Resistance Cellar.

Some failed. Desperate Dan and Meddlesome Matty and Strang the Terrible and Korky the Cat killed themselves with free gifts in a back room at the Peter Pan Club because they were impotent, like us. Their audience, the senile Chums of Red Circle School, still wearing for reasons of loyalty and lust the tatters of their uniforms, voted that exhibition a super wheeze.

Some succeeded. Tom Sawyer's heart has cooled, his ingenuity flowers at Cape Kennedy.

But they are all trodden on, the old familiar faces, so at the rising of the sun and the going down of the ditto I remember I remember the house where I was taught to play up play up and play the game though nobody told me what the game was, but we know now, don't we, we know what the game is, but lives of great men all remind us we can make our lives sublime and departing leave behind us arseprints on the sands of time, but the tide's come up, the castles are washed down, where are they now, where are they, where are the deep shelters? There are no deep shelters. Biggles may drop it, Worrals of the Wraf may press the button. So Billy and Bessie Bunter, prepare for the last and cosmic Yarooh and throw away the Man-Tan. The sky will soon be full of suns.

So Don't Feed Your Dog Ordinary Meat,
Feed Him Pal, Pal Meat for Dogs,
P-A-L, Prolongs Active Life
(Enriched with Nourishing Marrowbone Jelly)

My bird had a grin like a water-melon,
My bird was a hopeless case.
She wanted to look like Elvis Presley
So she paid a man to wipe the smile off her face,

He was
My friend the plastic surgeon
Your friend the plastic surgeon
Your friendly neighbourhood plastic surgeon
(Enriched with nourishing marrowbone jelly).

My mate was a dirty little Fascist,
They shouted him down when he cursed the Jews,
And nobody recognised his patriotic motives
Till he hired a man to explain his views,

He got
My friend the public relations man
Your friend the PRO
Your friendly neighbourhood public relations man
(Enriched with nourishing marrowbone jelly).

My dad was a nervy sort of navvy
He insured his job and his life and me
Fire, flood, suicide and acts of God,
And then he insured his insurance policy,

He paid
My friend the man from the Prudential
Your friend the man from the Pru
Your friendly neighbourhood man from the Prudential
(Enriched with nourishing marrowbone jelly).

My mum spent her life watching telly
Till the Epilogue told her that her soul would burn.
Now she's got peace of mind and she still does nothing
For she pays one-tenth of all we earn

To
My friend the Anglican clergyman
Your friend the clergyman
Your friendly neighbourhood Anglican clergyman
(Enriched with nourishing marrowbone jelly).

The plastic surgeon and the public relations man,
The man from the Prudential and the man from God –
Pals, pals, every one a pal.
P-A-L,
Prolongs Active Life
(Enriched with nourishing marrowbone jelly).

Time and Motion Study

Slow down the film. You see that bit.
Seven days old and no work done.
Two hands clutching nothing but air.
Two legs kicking nothing but air.
That yell. There's wasted energy there.
No use to himself, no good for the firm.
Make a note of that.

New film. Now look, now he's fourteen.
Work out the energy required
To make him grow that tall.
It could have been used
It could have all been used
For the good of the firm and he could have stayed small.
Make a note of that.

Age thirty. And the waste continues.
Using his legs for walking. Tiring
His mouth with talking and eating. Twitching.
Slow it down. Reproducing? I see.
All, I suppose, for the good of the firm.
But he'd better change methods. Yes, he'd better.
Look at the waste of time and emotion,
Look at the waste. Look. Look.
And make a note of that.

From Riches to Riches

The man of the people told the people he was one of them.
After five champagne years the people crowned him King of Phlegm.
High priest of steel and washing machines, see where Macmillan stands.
He who was conceived by the touching of two gloved hands.

Ode to Money

Man-eater, woman-eater, brighter than tigers,
Lover and killer in my pocket,
In your black sack I'm one of the vipers.
Golden-eyed mother of suicide,
Your photo's in my heart's gold locket.

You make me warm, you keep me cool,
You cure the terrifying dream.
Nature and art await your call.
Money, don't lead me to milk and honey
But a land of drambuie and icebergs of cream.

The Palm Court Planet's orchestra whines
The Money Spangled Money
And The Red Money. In my silver chains
I always stand when I hear the band
Play Money Save the Money.

Man at Large

Observe that man and see the lust
Bulging his serge as he cons a bust.
If he had to go cannibal he would eat
Only blonde secretarial meat.
His wife and his house and his brain are dim.
He didn't invent sex. Sex invented him.
He remembers a girl whose mouth was all
Like a cocktail cherry, and was smooth and cool.

Sulking down Wardour Street he goes,
Dreams in his head, corns on his toes.
But what would he do without feet? Fall down.
Where would he be without eyes? In a dark town.
Without hands? Unable to hold a knife,
A coin, a bottle or his wife.
Though his feet, eyes, hands, shuffle, stare and cling,
He falls down, is in the dark, cannot hold anything.

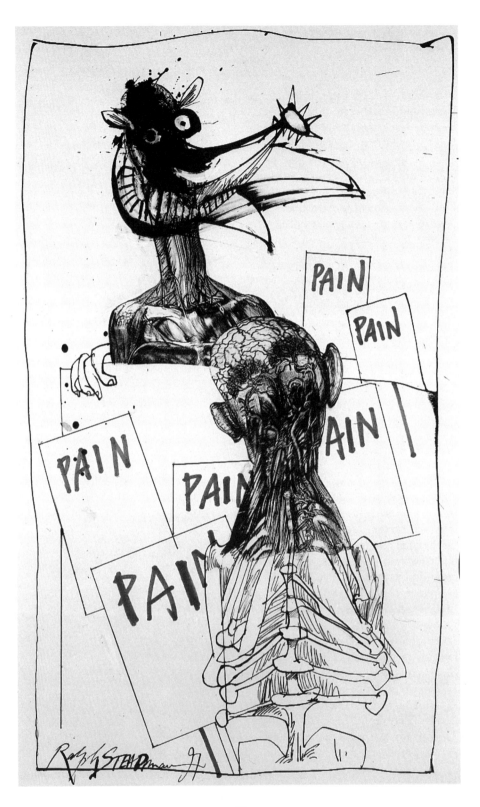

Fascist Speaker

Armoured like a rhinoceros
He hurls his tons into the crowd.
From half a dozen minds he rips
Triangles of flesh and blood.

Six shouts, six cardboard banners rise
Daubed with slogans saying Pain,
But wilt and tear in the hundredfold
Applause of men as mild as rain.

South Kensington Is Much Nicer

London, you hurt me. You're the girl
With hair fresh-permed and every curl
A gold ring in its proper place,
But spread across your poker face
A net of scars. A dress of smoke,
Your body an unfinished joke.
I love you, but I cannot sing
That money-splendoured hair is everything.
For I've walked through the alleys of Poison Town,
They led me up, they led me down.
The colour of the air was brown.

Reply to a Canvasser

Cats are spies for something dark.
Rabbits are wiped out.
Captain Cousteau scares the shark
With an underwater shout.

Snakes slide over jagged ground
Making the same sound as grass.
Elephants are pushed around.
Fish are hooked, or circle worlds of glass.

Hyenas have a nervous laugh,
Corruption is their only need.
Worms get fat, then cut in half.
A dog's a footman on a lead.

I'd rather be a stag at bay
Daubed in colours brown and gory,
Or any creature any day
Than be a bloody Tory.

Look at the View

Like the memory of a long-dead clerical uncle
Reclines St Paul's Cathedral
In the blue smoke from London's frying-pan.
Climb to the dome, and then you can
Watch the dull length of Blackfriars Bridge.
See the flat girl approach the edge,
Jump, fall, splash, vanish, struggle, cease.
Do you bet she'll be saved by the River Police
Who ride the tides in a humming launch?
Or an oil millionaire without a paunch
Will dive and take her wet to lunch?
Save her and leave her, and she'll be seen
Next day on the bridge near that tarnished tureen
St Paul's Cathedral, glowering in the rain.
She will take off her shoes and fall again.

The Beggar

The beggar shouts his martial wares:
'One bad eye and one wooden leg.
Now is the time for cash, not stares,
I am not rotting here to beg.
Who'll buy the north wind of the mind?
A fascinating pet. You'll find
   It's got a fist like a mallet
   Voice like a cistern
   Teeth like granite
   And an arm like a piston.
Sometimes it strays abroad for nights
But hunger brings it home. It bites
Only its master and his kind.
Your brain's the field, it is the mole.
Who buy my devil or my soul?'

'One wooden leg and one bad eye.
Then I danced, but now I flick
The woodlouse from my sewn-up thigh.
Watch them both and take your pick.
Once I was unique, alive.
Daubed with love you'd not believe.
 Then I saw the stars by day
 Looking from a well.
 Now the best that I can pray
 Is that my other eye should fail.
They sell you tickets to the moon,
I curse you with the sucking fly;
But who, bar me, hawks in this town
A dead branch and an evil eye?'

The Observer

A tattooed Irishman still
Shaking from his pneumatic drill.
 From his mouth
 Saunters sweet talk
 As he stretches the chained spoon
 To his mug of tea again.
Talk as sweet and warm as tea
Floats in bubbles from his mouth.
As he counts fivepence he's reminded
That his working life has ended.
Bubbles burst. His tongue's light tune
Stumbles and does not rise. Deep in his belly
The molten tea solidifies.
His tall face lowers slowly
Like a red wall collapsing in the rain.

A young Guards officer
Shaking with long-imprisoned anger.
 From his mouth
 Marches, in step, his conversation
 As he taps a silver plate
 With his menthol cigarette.
 Talk as white and soft as smoke
 Pours from his educated mouth.

His Colonel claims that the Brigade
Might well recruit the unemployed.
The young man's facial veins inflate,
His talk moves at the double, sweating,
Mad keen, but disciplined at that,
As his whole face opens letting
Free a smile bright as a bayonet.

In the café and the mess
A liberal hears what each man says.
   He notes the navvy's imagination
   And he smiles.
   Notes the Guard's well-drilled conversation
   And he smiles.
   With memories of Wimbledon
   He says under his pleasant breath:
   'Why don't both men just jump the net,
   Shake hands, and say the class war's won?'
   He lights a Woodbine from a Ronson.
   His eyes bulge, large with vision,
   Seeing both sides of every question,
   One with his left eye,
   One with his right,
   The cross-eyed, doomed hermaphrodite.

Solid Citizens

Let us praise the dead

Snug in their wooden homes
Under the aerials of Christ
Keeping themselves to themselves.

They do not strike or demonstrate;

Should they do so
They would lose the support
Of a sympathetic public.

Song About Mary

Mary sat on a long brown bench
Reading *Woman's Own* and *She*,
Then a slimy-haired nit with stripes on his collar
Said: 'What's the baby's name to be?'

She looked across to Marks and Spencers
Through the dirty window-pane,
'I think I'll call him Jesus Christ,
It's time he came again.'

The clerk he banged his ledger
And he called the Cruelty Man
Saying: 'This bird thinks she's the mother of Christ,
Do what you bleeding well can.'

They took Mary down to the country
And fed her on country air,
And they put the baby in a Christian home
And he's much happier there.

For if Jesus came to Britain
He would turn its dizzy head,
They'd nail him up on a telegraph pole
Or he'd raise the poor from the dead.

So if you have a little baby
Make sure it's legitimate child,
Bind down his limbs with insurance
And he'll grow up meek and mild.
    Meek and mild…meek and mild…meek and mild.

Dream Chant
(FROM *The Body*)

Dream about

electric wallpaper
hovercraft boots
blue suede robots and vertical take-off underwear

Dream about

dolphin steaks
nuclear umbrellas, bacteriological cigars
and package tours of the dark side of the Earth

Dream about

disposable children
jumbo-jet prostitutes
and Mantovani piped to the foetus in the womb

oh, vote for technology, my honey-pissing darling,
vote for Me.

We Call Them Subnormal Children
(FROM *The Body*)

They are here, they are here,
they are very far away.

Perhaps they see exciting visions
in the hollows of their hands.
Perhaps they can hear music we are deaf to
but I think their hearts trudge
and that their days trudge

for the way they sort of stand
the way they sort of speak

laboriously expresses one word only
wounded   wounded   wounded

We are taking a deep breath before the long slow dive through space to Mars.

We have not yet explored these island people.

They are here.
They will not go away.

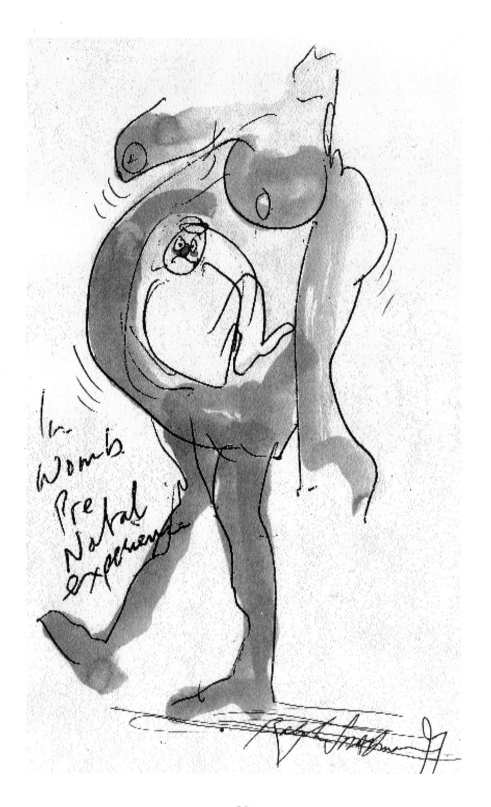

In
Womb.
Pre
Natal
experience

For a Medical Dictionary

Egghead

Your head becomes a soft-boiled egg.
Your hands' protective cradle rocks your forehead
And far inside, the restless baby,
The yolk,
Stirs.

Atmospheric Exdigestion

The patient is attacked from outside
By clusters of powerful farts
Attempting to get into him.

Festival

On Monday, with ceremonial ceremony
And a fanfare of funfairs,
We inaugurated
Be Kind To The Clitoris Week.
We finally found it
At 5.30 p.m. on Friday.

Final Chant
(FROM *The Body*)

Long live the child
Long live the mother and father
Long live the people

Long live this wounded planet
Long live the good milk of the air
Long live the spawning rivers and the mothering oceans
Long live the juice of the grass
and all the determined greenery of the globe
Long live the surviving animals
Long live the earth, deeper than all our thinking

31

We have done enough killing

Long live the man
Long live the woman
Who use both courage and compassion
Long live their children

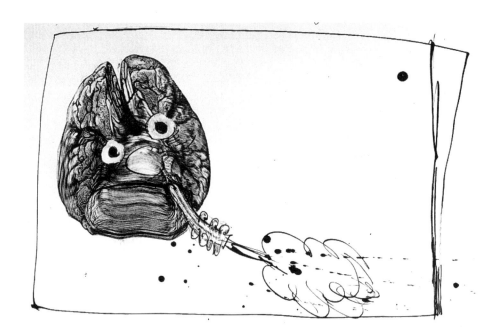

Early Shift on the *Evening Standard* News Desk

Fog Chaos Grips South

A thick blanket of fog lay across Southern England this morning like a thick
blanket –

'Don't let's call it a thick blanket today Joe, let's call it a sodden yellow
eiderdown.'

'Are you insane?'

In Other Words, Hold My Head

'Capitalism – ,' I started, but the barman hopped out of a pipkin.
'Capitalism,' he countered, 'that's a flat and frothless word.
I'm a good labourman, but if I mentioned capitalism
My clientèle would chew off their own ears
And spit them down the barmaid's publicised cleavage.'
'All right,' I obliged, 'don't call it capitalism,
Let's call it Mattiboko the Mighty.'

'Exploitation – ,' I typed, but the Editor appeared unto me,
A spike in one hand, a fiery pound note in the other.
'I'm a good liberal, but you're going out on a lamb –
You don't catch Burnem Levin writing about exploitation –
A million readers would gouge their eyes out,
Think of that, like two million pickled onions in the cornflakes.'
'Hold the back page,' I surlied, 'sod exploitation,
I'll retitle it The Massimataxis Incorporated Supplement.'

'Oppression and mass-murder – ,' I opined straight into the camera.
'Cut!' yelled the director, cutting off his head with a clapperboard.
'I'm a good fascist, but if you use that language
Half your viewers are going to
Tear the lids off their TV sets,
Climb inside, pour Horlicks over their heads
And die of calculated combustion.
Too late now to balance the programme
With a heartsofoak panel of our special experts
Who are all oppressors and mass-murderers.'
'You know the market,' I wizened,
'Oppression and mass-murder are out this year –
I'll christen them Gumbo Jumbo the Homely Obblestrog Spectacular.'

This was my fearless statement:
The Horror World can only be changed by the destruction of
Mattiboko the Mighty,
The Massimataxis Incorporated Supplement
And Gumbo Jumbo the Homely Obblestrog Spectacular.

Audience reaction was quite encouraging.

A Party Political Broadcast on Behalf of the Burial Party

SPOKESMAN:

Already our government has enforced the four freedoms:
Freedom to speak if you have nothing to say.
Freedom from fear if you stay in your shelter.
Freedom from want if you do what we want
And freedom from freedom.

But yesterday we, the British Government,
Detected, thanks to our spider's web of sundaypapers
And bloodshot radar traps,
Two mutineers scowling from your moderate ranks.

POLICE CONSTABLE BOOTHEAD:

At two in the morning I found the accused,
A man and a woman, both unclothed,
Sprawling across their mammoth bed.
(The mammoth is being held in custody at Disneyland.)
Their eyes were shut, and they grinned
Like a couple of pink grand pianos.
When asked why they were smiling with their eyes shut,
The accused informed me (in song):
'We are happy.'
I made a note of that at the time.

JUDGE:

What was that word again?

PROSECUTOR:

Happy, milord,
An expression common among delinquents.
It means – irresponsible.
Extensive chromosome and corpuscle counts,
Exhaustive spiritual testing
And a touch of the old Doctor Scholl revealed
That the male and female citizen were both addicted
To one of the most dangerous drugs on the list –
Exhibit A – Love –
Highly addictive, producing hallucinations,
For example:
Fats Waller fornicating downwards
At the wheel of a purple-striped cloud
To play *The Resurrection of South America* –

34

This love-drug can remove
The user's interest in moneyandproperty
And in killing in order to defend
Moneyandproperty.

JUDGE:
Stop it, I can't bear it.

SPOKESMAN:

The lovers were found guilty of not being guilty.
Their obscene craving was hard to cure
But a succession of secret licemen did their best.
They can hardly be blamed if the gasping lovers died
After ten days apart, ten days apart.
They died with their grins on, both of them drowned
In the same daydream,
The same degenerate lagoon.

Freedom to speak if you have nothing to say.
Freedom from fear if you stay in your shelter.
Freedom from want if you do what we want.
Freedom from freedom, freedom from sanity
And freedom, finally, from life.

IT IS LIKELY THAT DURING THE NEXT TEN YEARS
YOU WILL BE CALLED UPON TO DIE FOR FREEDOM.

Found Poem: An Englishman Comments on the Return of Roger Casement's Body to Ireland

That'll make room for one more nigger raging queer he was...

A Country Diary

As March melts into April, the jovial countryman breathes a sigh of relief which is visible from neighbouring farms. The winter's growth of ice, by now as thick as a blacksmith's thigh, has been carefully removed, a perfect disc, from the duckpond, and rolled without breakage to join the cylindrical pile of ice discs in the refrigerated silo. The last of the new-born lambs has been christened and tethered in his kennel of weather-chewed Yorkshire stone.

Spring bubbles in the jovial countryman's veins as he strides out, flame-thrower in hand, to rid the world of moles. On his wrist perches his faithful vulture, Tray.

The jovial countryman, face as red as a rabbit torn in half, spots Bob the Mole scurrying from scarecrow to scarecrow. Tray the Vulture registers a sharp intake of breath. Matt the Sheepdog flings aside his disguise. Cat the Cat raises a silhouetted claw against the bulbous scarlet of the seven p.m. sun. Crouch the Ferret clacks open and shut in the pocket of his master, the jovial countryman.

Bob the Mole flattens himself against a millstone. But it is not a millstone. Fergus the Tractor thunders down the flinty track, erupting through the coppice, regurgitating diesel in the form of rearward exhaust clouds, black clouds, death signals.

The serried animals jump upon Bob the Mole. Bob the Mole is dead. The feast over, all the animals return to their trenches. The jovial countryman plods down the lines, rewarding the good, punishing the bad.

Slogan Time

MEN ARE OUTNUMBERED BY TREES
THERE ARE EVEN MEAN MOUTHED WOMEN CALLED MOLLY
HOPE IN A THOUSAND YEARS
THE PISTOL WITH WHICH HITLER SHOT HIMSELF WAS VERY
        BEAUTIFUL
LONGING IS TOO LONG
FIGHT MADNESS WITH JOKES
JOAN OF ARC IS IRRELEVANT
EGGS ARE APPROVED BY THE DESIGN CENTRE
EVERY TIME AN MP OPENS HIS MOUTH – ANTS WALK OUT
GLOBAL FOOD RATIONING OR ARMAGEDDON

DREAMS ARE TOO SMALL TO SHARE
GET READY FOR CONSCRIPTION – LEARN TO SHOOT
CLERGY ARE PLAINCLOTHES MEN IN FANCY DRESS
THE MARRIAGE OF HEAVEN AND HELL IS OK, BUT WHAT ABOUT
      THE CHILDREN?

Dear Sir

I have read your Manifesto with great interest but it
says nothing about singing.

Press Photographs

Postage Stamp Exhibition

Outside the Central Hall, Westminster
the Lord Privy Seal releases a carrier pigeon
carrying a message of goodwill
to the Queen as a fellow stamp collector
to celebrate the fiftieth anniversary
of the Tasmanian Pigeon Post.

An old lady with a lace of driftwood
clutches the elbow of the Lord Privy Seal.
She tells him that she remembers
the Tasmanian Pigeon Post.

Podola

The day the cops got Podola.
In the wash-room a sub-editor says,
'He'll be getting a good going-over.'
Two sub-editors laugh
as they wash their hands with liquid soap
which smells of vomit.

Pat Boone

I am walking to interview Pat Boone
the Christian crooner
who would rather be dead
and his children dead and everything dead
than red.
I am thinking about Pat Boone
when a tree falls across the road with a long groan
and crushes my shadow.

Phone Call

I ring up an MP to ask about her illness.
She says she has cancer.
I tell her I am sorry.
She sounds as if she is smiling.
I tell her I am very sorry.

Just off Charing Cross Road There Are Alleys Full of Crocodiles

I'm dreaming about the fiscal year,
But I promise you, I promise you –
And I'll sharpen my forefinger to
A red-streaming ballpoint pen
So I can put this promise in writing you'll believe –
I don't want to live with Julie Andrews.

Warming my eyes in a bar.
The man on my left says Safe Deposit.
The lady on my right says Shirt.
Someone else says: You'd Think You'd
Get A Decent Life For A Pound A Head.

My Uncle Superhubert

My Uncle Superhubert's got no money, no sense, no heart, no hope.
But there's one thing everybody's got to admit, my Uncle Superhubert can cope.

Take the other week.

While the British Government was deciding whether to arm the white South
    Africans for purely economic reasons,
My Uncle closed the export gap by touring Rhodesia wearing only
    postage stamps commemorating the fiftieth birthday of the
    Soviet Secret Police.
When Uncle Superhubert heard about Otis Redding's death
He used Cliff Richard's halo to strangle Val Doonican's dentist.
When the newspapers announced that there was a split in the Liberal Party
He took out an after-life subscription to the *News Chronicle* and
laid snowballs on Gladstone's grave,
And when the bookies started taking bets on foot-and-mouth disease
My Uncle ran down to the Stock Exchange and bought a
controlling interest in leprosy.

No money, no sense, no heart, no hope –
But my Uncle Superhubert can cope.

Please Keep off the Dead

My Uncle Superhubert joined the Graveyard Police,
Says you couldn't wish for a sweeter manor.

Sometimes they hold a March of the Zombies,
But that's traditional, my Uncle leads them
Once round the boneyard and back to bed.

He gets the odd villain.
A couple of revolutionaries
Whose graves keep catching on fire
But mostly they're a decent mob, the dead.

Last week my Uncle went down to Gethsemane Corner
And rolled the stone away
And there was Bing Crosby
Singing *The Bells of St Mary's*.

Old Age Report

When a man's too ill or old to work
We punish him.
Half his income is taken away
Or all of it vanishes and he gets pocket-money.

We should reward these tough old humans for surviving,
Not with a manager's soggy handshake
Or a medal shaped like an alarm clock –
No, make them a bit rich,
Give the freedom they always heard about
When the bloody chips were down
And the blitz or the desert
Swallowed their friends.

Retire, retire into a fungus basement
Where nothing moves except the draught
And the light and dark grey figures
Doubling their money on the screen;
Where the cabbages taste like the mummy's hand
And the meat tastes of feet;
Where there is nothing to say except:
'Remember?' or 'Your turn to dust the cat.'

To hell with retiring. Let them advance.
Give them the money they've always earned –
or more – and let them choose.
We could wipe away some of their worry,
Some of their pain – what I mean
Is so bloody simple:
The old people are being robbed
And punished and we ought
To be letting them out of their cages
Into green spaces of enchanting light.

TV Talk

I thought it was about time we had a little chat. You know Charlie, he hates
pity. People who need people are the luckiest people in the world. We have
seen chaos and confusion, if I may use that expression. I think we've got to

rely on the decency and fair play of Rhodesians. I saw something from Heaven that made the sun look dim. There must be something else we can talk about, yes, prisons. It's his whole life, the game and what goes with it. Once you get beyond the Green Belt you may as well be in Timbuctoo. You're playing a very dangerous game, Delia. He's a rum bloke, that Mr Dodgson. Nobody's indispensable – nobody. Koala means: 'He does not drink. He really does not drink.' Sex is the mysticism of materialism. Let's get down the building site and cause a bit of damage. The pursuit of the goal must be unremitting and continuous. Coffee with Life In It. I have no aspirations in that area. Breakfast is an essential meal of which eggs are an essential part. If twenty ministers of the Church decided to go on the rampage, they could do just as much damage as twenty teenagers. Each one of the commercials is going to be a little parable. Well, how about that one, pop-pickers? We order our news editors to be objective. Getting married started when we went to look at furniture. Probably, like most other abuses, it's less than it seems. He's like a man in a trance – I don't think he's known much about it for the last four rounds. The still primitive passions of the people are mirrored in their faces. Few as one's readers may be, at least one knows they can read. Down every street there are folks like you and I. Yes, if it's limited to twenty megadeaths, we can accept that. Well there you are ladies, you can get another pair of curtains washed tomorrow...

Now We Are Sick

Christopher
          Robin
                    goes
                         hippety
immigrants   hoppety
          bring down
                    the value of
                              property

Involvement

QUESTION (from the *London Magazine*): In most European countries, and in America, writers are becoming involved, one way or another, in public manifestations of protest. As an English writer, do you feel that working on your own terms is more important than taking a practical part in organising public opinion?

In other words, in the continuing debates – about race, class, violence, war, financial priorities – that crucially affect our lives, are you for the writer in any way as polemicist, or do you believe that his instinct as an artist is ultimately the real test of his integrity?

ANSWER:

SCENE: an alley.

(*A* MAN *is being beaten up by* TWO POLICEMEN. *An* ENGLISH WRITER *approaches.*)

MAN: Help!

ENGLISH WRITER: Well, that may be what you think you want. But I've got to work on my own terms.

MAN: Help!

(TWO POLICEMEN put the boot in.)

ENGLISH WRITER: Look, I don't like this any more than you do. But I've got to follow my own instinct as an artist

MAN (*spitting teeth*): Yes, well that's ultimately the real test of your integrity.

(The beating up continues. ENGLISH WRITER pisses off to write a poem about ants.)

CURTAIN

Divide and Rule for as Long as You Can

Glasgow.
Trade Unionists march through the Square
Towards the City Chambers.

Police. Police. Police.

And in the streets leading off the Square –
Scottish soldiers with rifles.
Live ammunition.
They may be ordered to shoot into the crowd.

And behind the Scottish soldiers –
English soldiers with rifles.
Live ammunition.
If the Scottish soldiers refuse to shoot into the crowd
The English soldiers will be ordered
To shoot the Scottish soldiers.

Oh, but that was long ago.

That was in the future.

The Ballad of Sally Hit-and-Run

A train pulls into town and a woman jumps down
Her leathers are shining and her eyes are shining
With the body of a goddess and the cool of a nun
Everywhere she goes they call her Sally Hit-and-Run.

She moves down the street with a shuffle and a beat
Of her feet on the concrete – she's a creature
With senses that respond to every sound in town
And a hit-and-run habit when the sun goes down.

Sally Hit-and-Run on a barstool perch
Glances round the bar like a rector in church
Then she points one finger like a sensitive gun
And another guy topples to Sally Hit-and-Run.

Holiday Inn, Room three hundred and three,
Sally got him wrapped around the colour TV!
She shakes him and she bangs him like a tambourine,
Then she spreads him on the carpet like margarine.

Up comes the dawn – Sally's gone like a dream
Riding Inter-City drinking coffee and cream
Guy's left counting up the things he's done
Trying to give his goodness to Sally Hit-and-Run.

What Men Fear in Women

is as camouflaged
as a group of cougars
lying, perhaps,
among the spots of light and shadow
below a hot, astonishing tree

What Men Fear in Other Men

is as obvious
as the shining photographs
and cross-section diagrams
in a brochure provided,
with a smile, by a car salesman

English Scene

You sit at a table with two other men

Your left wrist slants in front of your throat
Your right incisors chew the nail on your left little finger
Your right index fingernail ploughs across the grain of the tabletop
You are nervous, obviously

You are right to be nervous, obviously

The man on one side of you has less money than you
He wants your money

The man on the other side of you has more money than you
He wants your money

Your left arm protects your throat
They usually go for the throat

A Warning

If you keep two angels in a cage
They will eat each other to death

Revolution

Its first shoots will burst out of the earth
silently, at the wrong time of year
in a silent part of the island
far from the patrolling armoured cars.

A finger, pointing towards the sun,
which will be mistaken for a blade of grass
if anybody notices it at all.

One deep night, an armoured division
returning from an easy mission
in Leicester or in Birmingham
will be crushed by the branches
of the numberless, nameless trees
of an overnight forest.

And those breeding trees
with eccentric outlines
will be no more like our theories
than a hippopotamus
is like a parallelogram.

Under Photographs of Two Party Leaders, Smiling

These two smiled so the photographer
Could record their smiles
FOR YOU

As they smiled these smiles
They were thinking all the time
OF YOU

They smile on the rich
They smile on the poor
They smile on the victim in his village
They smile on the killer in his cockpit

Yes, Mummy and Daddy
Are smiling, smiling
AT YOU

please try to smile back.

Ancestors

We had an island.
Oh we were a stomping old tribe on an island.
Red faces, hairy bodies.
Happy to be hairy
Happy to be hairy
When the breezes tickled
The hairs of our bodies
Happy to be hairy
Happy to be hairy
Next best thing to having feathers –
That was our national anthem.
Right. Hairy tribe,
Hairy red story-telling, song-singing, dragon-fighting, fire-drinking tribe.

Used to get invaded every other weekend.
Romans, Vikings, Celts – fire and sword –
Pushed us back but they never broke us down.
In between invasions we grew spuds and barley,
Took our animals wherever there was a river and some grass.

When the snows came, we moved south
When the rivers dried, we moved west
When the invaders came, we burnt our crops, moved.

Until one day we were surrounded by warriors
The same old fire and sword, but used efficiently.
They slaughtered our warriors, lined up the rest of us
And there were speeches
About law and order, and firm but fair government.

And this is what they did,
This is government.
You take an island and cut it carefully
With the razorblade called law and order
Into a jigsaw of pieces.
The big, rich-coloured pieces
Go to the big, rich men.
The smaller, paler pieces,
(Five beds two recep barn mooring rights five acres)
Go to the small, rich men.
And nothing at all
Goes to those who have nothing at all.

Absurd? The many nothing-at-alls
Wouldn't stand back and see their island
Slashed into ten thousand pieces.
They didn't stand back, our hairy tribal ancestors.
Some of them spoke out. Some fought back.
They were slashed down by the giant razorblade.

And now, and now the rich seldom have to kill
To defend the land they stole from all the tribe –
Wire fences. Guard Dogs Loose on these Premises. No Trespassing.
Bailiffs. Security Guards. Police. Magistrates Courts. Judges. Prison –
Grey prisons where the brain and the flesh turn grey
As the green English years stroll by outside the walls.
So who needs fire and sword?
The tribe has been tamed
And our island
Our daft green stony gentle rough amazing haven
Entirely surrounded by fish
Has been stolen from the tribe.
It was robbery with most bloody violence.
And that was history, history is about the dead.
Then is our tribe dead? Is our tribe dead?
Is the tribe dead?

Saw It in the Papers

Her baby was two years old.
She left him, strapped in his pram, in the kitchen.
She went out.
She stayed with friends.
She went out drinking.

The baby was hungry.
Nobody came.
The baby cried.
Nobody came.
The baby tore at the upholstery of his pram.
Nobody came.

She told the police:
'I thought the neighbours would hear him crying,
and report it to someone who would come
and take him away.'

Nobody came.

The baby died of hunger.

She said she'd arranged for a girl,
whose name she couldn't remember,
to come and look after the baby
while she stayed with friends.
Nobody saw the girl.
Nobody came.

Her lawyer said there was no evidence
of mental instability.
But the man who promised to marry her
went off with another woman.

And when he went off, this mother changed
from a mother who cared for her two-year-old baby
into a mother who did not seem to care at all.
There was no evidence of mental instability.

The Welfare Department spokesman said:
'I do not know of any plans for an inquiry.
We never become deeply involved.'
Nobody came.
There was no evidence of mental instability.

When she was given love
she gave love freely to her baby.
When love was torn away from her
she locked her love away.
It seemed that no one cared for her.
She seemed to stop caring.
Nobody came.
There was no evidence of mental instability.

Only love can unlock locked-up-love.

Manslaughter: She pleaded Guilty.
She was sentenced to be locked up
in prison for four years.

Is there any love in prisons?

She must have been in great pain.

There is love in prisons.
There is great love in prisons.
A man in Gloucester Prison told me:
'Some of us care for each other.
Some of us don't.
Some of us are gentle,
some are brutal.
All kinds.'

I said: 'Just the same as people outside.'
He nodded twice,
and stared me in the eyes.

What she did to him was terrible.
There was no evidence of mental instability.
What was done to her was terrible.
There is no evidence of mental instability.

Millions of children starve, but not in England.
What we do not do for them is terrible.

Is England's love locked up in England?
There is no evidence of mental instability.

Only love can unlock locked-up love.

Unlock all of your love.
You have enough for this woman.
Unlock all of your love.
You have enough to feed all those millions of children.

Cry if you like.
Do something if you can. You can.

Ten Ways to Avoid Lending Your Wheelbarrow to Anybody

1 *Patriotic*

May I borrow your wheelbarrow?
I didn't lay down my life in World War II
so that you could borrow my wheelbarrow.

2 *Snobbish*

May I borrow your wheelbarrow?
Unfortunately Samuel Beckett is using it.

3 *Overweening*

May I borrow your wheelbarrow?
It is too mighty a conveyance to be wielded
by any mortal save myself.

4 *Pious*

May I borrow your wheelbarrow?
My wheelbarrow is reserved for religious ceremonies.

5 *Melodramatic*

May I borrow your wheelbarrow?
I would sooner be broken on its wheel
and buried in its barrow.

6 *Pathetic*

May I borrow your wheelbarrow?
I am dying of schizophrenia
and all you can talk about is wheelbarrows.

7 *Defensive*

May I borrow your wheelbarrow?
Do you think I'm made of wheelbarrows?

8 *Sinister*

May I borrow your wheelbarrow?
It is full of blood.

9 *Lecherous*

May I borrow your wheelbarrow?
Only if I can fuck your wife in it.

10 *Philosophical*

May I borrow your wheelbarrow?
What is a wheelbarrow?

Vroomph! *or* The Popular Elastic Waist

(A cut-up of sentences from the Sunday Times Colour Magazine of 9 December 1967, which featured Civil Defence, Famous Footballers, The Girls of Thailand, Gangsters, and several advertisements.)

Juliet sighs. Romeo speaks.

Deep shelters are out of most people's reach.

The white tin is a simple gadget for pinpointing the size and position of
    nuclear bursts.

Simply push the needle in, pump the handle, and

You haven't seen anything till you've seen the 200 pounds of beautiful Louise

Tucked away in the secret, hardened, national seat of government,

Or balanced on bicycles while removing 12 shirts.

Yet, even when we made love, at a time when most
        women are feeling romantic, she would start to
             prattle away about

The Royal State Trumpeters of the Household Cavalry.

Stimulated by these breaks in the nuclear overcast,
        the Sunday Times here offers what is probably the
            first complete review of our Civil Defence
                preparations,

A symbol of the virile, aggressive, muscular game which
        one associates with a man who has twice broken the
            same leg – and twice returned to the game.

This is the problem: whether to drink Cointreau neat
        and slowly savour every warming sip,

Or hang from the tops of palm trees by our feet.

While we have the bomb it seems ridiculous not to be honest.

It works like this: the motor is powered by ordinary torch batteries.

The slightly wounded will be sent on their way, the severely wounded left to

The Marquis de Ferrara.

Fill out the Panic Sheet.

Neither the Sunday Times nor its agents accepts any liability for loss or

The gruesome electric chair.

You see, we are unashamedly devoted to the kind
      of quiet courtesy
           which gets rarer
                every
                    day.

Leaflets

(for Brian Patten and my twelve students at Bradford)

Outside the plasma supermarket
I stretch out my arm to the shoppers and say:
'Can I give you one of these?'

I give each of them a leaf from a tree.

The first shopper thanks me.
The second puts the leaf in his mack pocket where his wife won't see.
The third says she is not interested in leaves. She looks like a mutilated willow.
The fourth says: 'Is it art?' I say that it is a leaf.
The fifth looks through his leaf and smiles at the light beyond.
The sixth hurls down his leaf and stamps it till dark purple mud oozes through.
The seventh says she will press it in her album.
The eighth complains that it is an oak leaf and says he would be on my side if
I were also handing out birch leaves, apple leaves, privet leaves and larch leaves.
I say that it is a leaf.
The ninth takes the leaf carefully and then, with a backhand fling, gives it its
    freedom.
It glides, following surprise curving alleys through the air.
It lands. I pick it up.
The tenth reads both sides of the leaf twice and then says: Yes, but it doesn't
    say who we should kill.'

But you took your leaf like a kiss.

They tell me that, on Saturdays,
You can be seen in your own city centre
Giving away forests, orchards, jungles.

Midnight Mary from Llandudno

Midnight Mary from Llandudno
stomped in the bar and ordered vinegar and water
vinegar and water.

She beat out her heartbeat on the photo of a baby –
My husband was the root of all evil.
I want vinegar and water.

She rocked from her thighs, rocked from her hips
and she slapped out the rhythm with her flat old feet
but they wouldn't give her any vinegar and water.

Well thank you for the vinegar and water.
Thank you for the vinegar and water.
Thank you for the vinegar and water.

SLAM

World Cup Song
(for the Scottish team)

Kick that football
Like you kick your mother
Kick that football
Like you kick your wife
Kick that football
Like you kick your children

Footballs never kick back

The Obliterating Prizes

A gruesome occurrence fell on me once
   When I was a sammy at oxford
They chose me to be the college's dunce
   O I was the lubber of oxford

A conical hat they plunked on my head
   Those grievous old gories in oxford
With a D for Dunce wrote upon it in red
   Yes I was downderried at oxford

Now underbred dunderheads romp round the town
   Through the blithering weather of oxford
Each wears a gold cap and a silvery gown
   Each moocher but adrian in oxford

And I cautiously watch their regalia flap
   As I stand in the corner in oxford
For now I've been wearing that overhead hat
   For twenty dark blue years of oxford

Illumination

By the light of
Thirty forks of forty-pronged
Infra-blue lightning
Fifty forks of sixty-pronged
Infra-white lightning

I saw a bright transparent range of mountains
Stamp in a circle of dance round Birmingham

The rocks shook to the drums of waterfalls

The million trumpets of the sun
Disgorged their gold

Gold

Gold

Till the whole world was gold

Ode to Enoch Powell

The vulture is an honest man
He offers no apology
But snaps the fingers from the hand
And chews them with sincerity

Birmingham Council are bidding for the Berlin Wall.
There's swastikas sprouting in the ground round Bradford Town Hall
Callaghan and Thatcher are dancing cheek to cheek –
Everybody getting ready for Kindness to Vultures Week

The vulture is a gentleman
He does not stoop to kill
But watches murders from a height
Then drops to eat his fill

The Press is so excited that the Press can hardly speak
There's red stuff dripping from the corner of the *Telegraph*'s beak.
You can say that white is right but it looks like black is bleak
Everybody getting ready for Kindness to Vultures Week.

The vulture is a Christian man
Goes to church on Sunday
Prays to God to give him strength
To tear a corpse on Monday...

But when Mr Enoch Powell
Emigrates from this life
And the media forget to mention
That his tongue was a poison knife
When they lay him out in state
With a lipstick job
And an aura of after-shave
And twenty-one guns have farted Goodbye –
We'll dance on the bugger's grave

Dance on the earth that's hotter than his life
His blood was chilled
Dance to the music of the human beings
That liar killed

We'll stomp – 1, 2, 3, 4, 5, 6
Stomp – 7, 8, 9, 10.
Yes we'll stomp all night till the soil's right tight
So Enoch never rises again.

The Blackboard

Five foot by five foot,
(The smalls have measured it.)
Smooth black surface,
(Wiped by a small after every class.)
Five different colours of chalk
And a class of thirty-five smalls,
One big.

Does the big break up the chalk
Into thirty-five or thirty-six
And invite the smalls to make
A firework show of colours
Shapes and words
Starting on the blackboard
But soon overflowing
    All over the room
    All over the school
    All over the town
    All over the country
    All over the world?

    No.
The big looks at the textbook
Which was written by a big
And published by a big.
The textbook says
The names and dates of Nelson's battles.
So the big writes, in white,
Upon the black of the blackboard,
The names and dates of Nelson's battles.
The smalls copy into their books
The names and dates of Nelson's battles.

    Nelson was a big
Who died fighting for freedom or something.

Question Time in Ireland

1. If the Devil had used all his ingenuity to damn Ireland, could he have in-
   vented a more devastating trinity than the Roman Catholic Church, the
   Protestant Church and the English Houses of Parliament?

2. Why is it possible to withdraw from India, Kenya and Aden – but impossible to withdraw from Ireland?

3. Did Jesus say: Blessed are the poor, for they shall tear each others' throats out? Blessed are the rich, for they shall watch the tearing out of the throats and shall place bets upon the outcome?

4. What's wrong with torture in a good cause so long as it's not reported on television?

5. What is the answer to the English Question?

The Savage Average

I feel like a little girl of six
In a school built of two hundred thousand bricks
And every day, in the purple playground,
One child is chosen and killed by the other children.

Small Adventure

Walked over the hill.
Stood looking down into a valley
shining full of a million million
ball-point pens.

What It Means To Be a Man in London

Down London canyons move the high-tension
cowboys, gangsters, boxers and rockstars
         iron mouths   frozen eyes
      tougher you look   safer you are

saw a snowdrop in the park
kicked it to death
felt really ballsy

Barred from Every Decent Pub

there was an old man who was ill in the head
he filled the people of the town with dread
they cried he is ill he is ill in the head
but he was only ill in the head

Have Another

I made my palms into a waterbowl,
   you lowered your head and drank.
A dozen dips for your dusty lips
   but you gave me no irrigated thanks.
You said: That can't be a lake you're giving me –
   a lake has got to have banks.

Closing Time

The whole point of the sun
   is there's so much for the sun to shine on
The whole point of the sun
   is there's so much for the sun to shine on
But when there's nothing left to warm up
   he'll just pack his golden bags and be gone

It All Shines

Two magpies
Hopping on and off
That old stone pigsty

Their white feathers
Are shining well
What else are white feathers
Supposed to do but shine

Yes but their black feathers too
Shining shining black
Black rays of light to my eyes
And that was news to me

Yes
Black and White
Green Yellow Blue Red
Brown Purple Orange
Stone Earth Grass
Wood Wire Paint
Hens Trees Sky Gravel
Everything I can see
From this shining window
Shines

Men rocketed out into emptiness
They took a long look back
The earth was shining at them
The earth was shining

Of course

It all shines
It all shines

Loose Leaf Poem

(This is a diary of good and bad things, mostly for friends and allies but with a few sections for enemies as well. It was written in a peaceful room with a view of the Yorkshire Dales. In reading it aloud, I often change the order of sections, talk in between sections and leave out any part which doesn't seem relevant at the time.)

*

There was a child danced with a child
The music stopped

*

I stopped reading The Wretched of the Earth
Because you cannot read it all the time.

My stomach felt like outer space.
The sunday papers all sounded
Like bidders in a slave market.

I ate rapidly, alone,
Because I couldn't sit and eat with anyone,
Or look at anyone.

I glanced into the television's eye.
it was both bright and blind.

I was full of useless tears.
I did not use them

*

Who was the hooligan who ripped off all your skin, madam?
The North Atlantic Treaty Organisation.

*

Below my window, a stone wall begins,
swerves past a tree, drags its weight
upwards, almost collides with a second tree,
breaks for a gate, resumes,
and skitters over the horizon.
I watch the way it rides,
blonde stone in the blonde light of Yorkshire.

*

Are you bored by pictures of burning people?
You will be bored to death.

They did the dying.
You did nothing.

Not a gesture, not a word, not a breath,
Not a flicker of one line of your face.

You said: There is nothing I can do.
As you said it you seemed so proud.

*

There was a wretched danced with a wretched
The music began to burn.

*

In the chapel-cold porridge of fear
Crouched the spirit of Edward Lear
   Through the hole in his head
   His agony bled
   Till he changed to a Whale
   And spouted a hail –
Cholomondley Champagne and the best Babylonian Beer.

*

To   Ian Hamilton and A. Alvarez, Poetry Reviewers –
   Get your blue hands
   off the hot skin of poetry

*

(to dogmatic men and automatic dogs)

I'm an entrist, centrist, Pabloite workerist
– Sweet Fourth International and never been kissed,
I've got a mass red base that's why I'd rather sit on the floor,
If you want to be a vanguard, better join Securicor.

My daddy was opportunistic
My mama was mystified
I want to be a movement
But there's no one on my side...

NO REVOLUTION WITHOUT COMPASSION
NO REVOLUTION WITHOUT COMPASSION

*

Never look out
You might see something bigger than you
Never go out
You might get your iambics dirty

Wine is a river
Flowing down to sleep
So climb in the boat
With your legitimate wife
No sharks   No storms
No underwater explosions

Never look out
The sun might punch you in the eye –

Say home.

*

I pulled on my solid granite gargoyle suit, borrowed a hunch from
    Sherlock Holmes and swung down from the turrets of Notre
        Dame just in time to rescue the naked Andromeda who was
            chained to King Kong in the middle of Red Square,
                Milwaukee.

Mark Antony immediately denounced me to a mob of Transylvanian
    peasants, who hurried me to the nearest oasis for a good
        guillotining.

Luckily for me the Flying Nun was power-diving down for a
    suicide raid on Moby Dick.

She noticed my plight, shot out a tentacle and scooped me into an
    echo chamber full of Dusty Springfields, thus foiling the
        machinations of Edgar Allen Fu Manchu, the Jackdaw of Zenda.

So you will understand why I am delighted to be here tonight to
    introduce a fourth member of fiction's Trolleybus Trinity –
        ladies and gentlemen, let's hear it for Miss Marlene Brontë.

*

At the end of each adventure
Mighty Mouse stands, arms folded, on a pedestal,
Cheered by a crowd of infant mice.

Every Sunday
God is praised
In several million churches.

Mighty Mouse saved us from the Monster Cat!!!!

                    *

In case the atmosphere catches on fire
The first thing to do will be to burn

My brain socialist
My heart anarchist
My eyes pacifist
My blood revolutionary

                    *

The man who believes in giraffes would swallow anything.
There's been nothing about ostriches in the papers for months,
      somebody's either building an ostrich monopoly or
      herding them into concentration camps.
Butterflies fly zigzag because they want to fly zigzag.
I have looked into a hedgehog's face and seen nothing but goodness.
A huge ram stamps his foot – a million sheep charge and occupy
      the Bradford Wool Exchange.

                    *

            pip
            pop
            pip
            pop
     pip   pip   pip
            pop

i am either a sound poet
or a bowl of Rice Crispies

                    *

(to a friend who killed himself)

All that pain
double-bulging under your forehead
I wish you could have taken
a handful of today's Yorkshire snow
and pressed it to that pain.
You rummaged for peace
in the green country, in the eye of the sun,
in visions of Tibet,
brain-shaking drugs, black magic,
police stations, among the stones,
beneath the stones.
But the stones, which seemed so calm,
screamed into life in your hurt hands.
Simpler than you
I simply wish you were alive
walking among this snowfall.
I'm glad that all your pain is dead.

*

Your breath is like deodorant, your blood like Irish lager,
Your idea of paradise an infinite Forsyte Saga,
Your head belongs to Nato and your heart to the Playboy Club,
You're the square root of minus zero, playing rub-a-dub-dub in a Fleet Street pub.

Sit tight in your tower of money...

You've got a problem of identity, ooh what an intellectual shame,
You've got a million pseudonyms and can't recall your maiden name,
You cannot tell your face from your arse or your supper from your sex,
But you always remember who you are when it comes to signing cheques –

Sit tight in your tower of money...

In case England catches on fire
The first thing to do will be to form a committee
To organise a weekend seminar
On Little-Known Conflagrations in Italian History
Or The Rise and Fall of the Safety Match in Literature and Life.

*

Many thin men
saying: No.

But of course we've got to inside-out ourselves
and splash around in our own juice,
and the juice can't shine if you don't throw it up into the light,
and of course you're hard to hit if you keep dancing
and harder to hit if you make up your own dance as you dance,
and of course Tarzan is more exciting than Anthony Trollope
because he can MOVE, swinging through jungles of clubfooted prose,
into your eye and out your navel,
and of course there's no perfect music,
no perfect words,
only the ridiculous beauty of man and woman
silly with each other,
pulling off their skins and swinging them round their heads,
becoming incredible fountains upon legs –

Many thin men
saying: No.

*

There's a factory for making factories,
A sinking pool for learning to drown,
A university like a pencil sharpener
To whittle you down to a pinpoint.
There's a mean old weather machine
Churning out crapstorms
And a generation gap between
Me and what I used to be.
But the cities of horror,
Skull pavements, murder girders –
They're going to crumble away in our hands.

*

The ice-cubes in my bloodstream decided to melt today.
I'd buy a moustache like everyone else
But I'm too attached to golden syrup.
There are hailstones big as hailstones, but I'm sure
They're not aimed at me.
Yes, Timbuctoo. I suddenly want to go to Timbuctoo.

*

Grass pours down the hillside.
The stone wall gradually turns green.
A dead tree can keep its balance for years.

                              *

You can't win
Mary Queen of Scots invented high-heel shoes to make her-
self look taller they cut her bloody head off. (John Walton)

                              *

Suddenly it hits me that it's May Day and I hadn't even noticed it was April,
And was gazing over the floodlit fields at a group of socially-minded cows,
And laughing to myself about the time Allen Ginsberg bared his arse to the
     people in a whizzing-by train,
And marking passages in a book of Fidel Castro's speeches –
Quote – And then you hear a revolutionary say: They crushed us,
They organised 200 radio programmes, so many newspapers,
     so many magazines, so many TV shows,
     so many of this and so many of that – and one wants to ask him,
What did you expect?
That they would put TV, radio, the magazines, the newspapers,
     the printing shops –
All this at your disposal?
Or are you unaware that these are the instruments of the ruling class
Designed explicitly for crushing the Revolution? – unquote.
And I was also thinking of the pirhana fish grinning in the depths of my bank
     manager's soul,
And I was looking through the BBC Folk Club magazine and trying to
     imagine the BBC Folk,
And I was looking forward to a bit of bed with Celia in the afternoon,
And my eyes kept returning to a letter from the poet Tim Daly,
Liquid blue handwriting between strict blue lines,
His words saying – quote –
As a whole, the support I have received has amazed me,
I had anticipated only antagonism.
Love be praised, I was wrong – unquote –
And I look again at his address:
Her Majesty's Prison, County Road, Maidstone, Kent.
Tim, aged twenty-one, who took his petrol bombs
To the Imperial War Museum
Because the Museum was teaching children war...
And so when it suddenly hits me that it's been May Day all day
And I should be feeling solidarity,
I think yes so I should, and yes I do, and so yes I write this down

As a demonstration of solidarity –
With the cows, who have now moved on,
With Allen Ginsberg, who has now moved on,
With Fidel Castro as he moves socialism onwards,
With Celia who moves me as we move together,
And with Tim Daly the poet,
Locked away for four years
So that England may be safe for the dead.

Back in the Playground Blues

I dreamed I was back in the playground, I was about four feet high
Yes dreamed I was back in the playground, standing about four feet high
Well the playground was three miles long and the playground was five miles wide

It was broken black tarmac with a high wire fence all around
Broken black dusty tarmac with a high fence running all around
And it had a special name to it, they called it The Killing Ground

Got a mother and a father, they're one thousand years away
The rulers of The Killing Ground are coming out to play
Everybody thinking: 'Who they going to play with today?'

    Well you get it for being Jewish
    And you get it for being black
    Get it for being chicken
    And you get it for fighting back
    You get it for being big and fat
    Get it for being small
    Oh those who get it get it and get it
    For any damn thing at all

Sometimes they take a beetle, tear off its six legs one by one
Beetle on its black back, rocking in the lunchtime sun
But a beetle can't beg for mercy, a beetle's not half the fun

I heard a deep voice talking, it had that iceberg sound
'It prepares them for Life' – but I have never found
Any place in my life worse than The Killing Ground.

December Cat

Among the scribbled tangle
of the branches of that garden tree
only about two hundred
lime-coloured leaves still shudder

but the hunting cat
perched in the middle of the scribble
believes he's invisible
to the few sparrows visiting
the tips of the tree

like a giant soldier
standing in a grey street at noon
wearing a bright ginger uniform
hung with guns
hung with grenades
who holds a sprig of heather up
as he shouts to the houses:
Come out! It's all right,
I'm only a hillside!

The Swan

The anger of the swan
Burns black
Over ambitious eyes.

The power of the swan
Flexes steel wings
To batter feeble air.

The beauty of the swan
Is the sermon
Preached between battles.

Farm Animals

Clotted cream sheep
We troop in a dream
Through the steep deep wool
Of a yellow meadow
We are oblong and boring
We are all alike
Liking to be all alike

And the grass-like grass
Is alike, all alike, and all we think
Is grass grass grass
Yes grass is all we think
And all we do
Is wool

But that's the deal, the ancient deal,
The wonderful deal between sheep and men

Men give grass
We come across with wool

That agreement was signed
On the green baize table in Eden

What would happen if we broke the contract?
Oh that would be mutiny, we would be punished
By being eaten, we would deserve to be eaten.
But of course we never rebel, so we are never eaten.

On the Verses Entitled 'Farm Animals'

The stereotypical tra-a-avesty opposite
Purports to speak for sheep
Nothing could be more cra-a-assly human

Despite our similar coiffures
Each sheep's a separate planet
With its own opinions and visions

All that we share is the furnace heart
Of all long-distance serfs
We're hot and getting hotter
So shepherds, you better watch your flocks

A. Ram

The Owl Song

(after watching a terrible battle, Merlin decides to live as an owl in a wood)

I have walked through the valley of slate
And the rain was blue
I have seen the sky like a hunter's net
Deepest darkest blue
I have seen the bit tight in the horse's teeth
And the bit was blue
I have heard swords sing on the battlefield
And the swords were blue
I have seen the eyes of my dead foe
They were round as the world and blue
I have seen the face of my friend in the dawn
On the sheep-shorn grass – his face was blue
    Blue grave
  Blue gravel on a grave
Blue flowers on the gravel on a grave

And I shall wake in the blue night
And sleep in the blue day
And I will live my own blue life
In the blue tree   In the blue tree

And my food shall be blue
And my wine shall be blue
And my mind shall be filled
With nothing but blue

blue blue   blue blue   blue blue

Commuting the Wrong Way Round Early Morning

Caught the Gospel Oak train
At the dog-end of Tuesday night.
Camden Town darkness
Laying like gravy on a plate...
But at Liverpool Street Station
They've got a smudgey brand of blue daylight.

Here comes half the Essex population
Tensed up for their desky work.
I'm struggling up a waterfall –
Bubbling secretaries, rocky clerks.
For I'm off to Billericay
Like a sausage on a fork.

For My Son

'The next best thing to the human tear'
ADVERTISING SLOGAN FOR AN EYEWASH

The next best thing to the human tear
Is the human smile
Which beams at us reflected white
For a lunar while.
But smiles congeal. Two eyes alight
With water cannot glow for long,
And a better thing than the human tear
Is the human song.

If cigarette or city burn
The smoke breaks into air.
So your breath, cries and laughter turn
And are abandoned there.
Once I had everything to learn
And thought each book had pretty pages.
Now I don't even trust the sun
Which melts like butter through the ages.

Nevertheless, crack-voiced I'll sing
For you, who drink the generous light
Till, fat as happiness, you sing
Your gay, immortal appetite.
I bring you air, food, grass and rain,
Show you the breast where you belong.
You take them all and sing again
Your human song.

Brazil Nut in Edinburgh

Strapping upon her head the brand-new sporran
Dolores hoped she did not look too foreign

Four Sorry Lines

Sixteen years old, and you would sneer
At a baby or a phoenix.
Mock on, mock on, in your blue-lidded splendour –
Most well-paid jobs are reserved for cynics.

Action and Reaction Blues

Further back you pull a bow-string
    the further the arrow goes whooshin
Further back Maggie drags us
    the further the revolution

Screws and Saints

What's worse than the uniformed devils
When they trap you in a concrete hell?
The claws and boots of the angels
When you're savaged in a golden cell.

Nearly Nothing Blues

Well it's six o'clock and I done nearly nothing all day
Yes 6 p.m. – done nearly nothing all day
I'll do half as much tomorrow if I get my way

New Skipping Rhymes

Good little Georgie
Worked like a madman
Three years at Oxford
Five years an Adman
Went on Mastermind
Did so well on that show
Now he's the Host
Of a TV Chat Show

> My savings are my baby
> Money is my boss
> My mummy and my daddy
> Were profit and loss
> One thousand, two thousand, three
> thousand, four…

Meat on the hook
Powder in the jar
Mickey Jagger is a Star
S-T-A-R spells Star
He can whistle
He can hum
He can wriggle his umpumbum

> Pretty little Pam
> Passed her exam
> What shall we give her?
> Doughnuts with jam
>
> Stupid little Sam
> Failed his exam
> What shall we give him?
> Who gives a damn?

The High School Bikeshed

Yellow stairs
Do the zig-zag stagger.
In the red shed
The bikes are snogging.
Silver, they whisper to each other,
Silver, silver.

Staying Awake

Monday came so I fucked off to school
School is a big huge building
Where you're not supposed to get any fucking sleep
We hung around till they counted us in a room
With pictures of fucking owls and bats
Then we hung around some more

Miss Harburton ponced in and yelled about
How her fucking bike's gone missing who cares
Then we all fucked off to another room

It was Mister Collins from Outer Space
Talked about not leaving gum stuck around
And Queen Victoria up the Suez Canal
And how he wouldn't let us act out
The Death of General Gordon again
Not ever and no he never saw *Chainsaw Massacre*
And no didn't want to even free
On Goodgeman's sexy mother's video
And Beano Black said his mother was poorly
And started to give us the fucking grisly details
Saved by the bell and we hung around
Smoking in the bog and not getting any sleep

Then we all fucked off to another room
And it was Mrs Grimes Environmental Studies
So I finally got my fucking sleep.

I stay out of trouble but in my head
I'm bad I'm fucking bad as they come
When I die they'll punish me
For the things I done in my fucking head.
They'll send me off to a big huge building
And they won't let me get any fucking sleep.
Well that's what I reckon
Death is like fucking off
To another fucking school.

Bring Out Your Nonsense

A detective-sergeant walks into the police station
A woman with a floor at home inspects the carpet store
A train stops at the platform after deceleration
Librarians enter the library through the library door
Telephonists at the switchboard are answering telephones
A *Telegraph* reader buys the *Telegraph* from the paper shop
Cars drive, pedestrians walk and my heart groans
As out of the Billericay copshop steps a cop

But I'm wrong – the cop debags himself to give birth to a phoenix
Which zips down the High Street with Dizzy Gillespian squeals
And the silver and gold melts in all the jewellers' windows
And the town is crotch-deep in whirlpools of syrup
And you sail over the horizon in a pea-blue schooner
Bearing the wild good news you sail bearing the good wild food
Over the horizon with a ton of friends playing magical banjoes
And the people of Billericay dance in delirious dozens

Reassuring Song if Your Name Is Mitchell

A million Mitchells sing this song
A million Mitchells can't be wrong
We are a million Mitchells strong
Why don't you just sing along?
Why don't you just sing along?
    Happy-go-zombie,
    Hello Abercrombie!
With a million marching Mitchells

All Darks Are Alike in the Death

As you crouch on my chest
I'll stroke your fur
Funny old death
Purr   purr   purr   purr

Buy a Sprig of Haggis for Bad Luck, Sir?

Have you ever been pregnant on Euston Station?
And they said you'd be met at your destination
By a fixer who'd be wearing an Asian carnation
And you stare around the concourse in consternation
For it's the annual outing of the Royal Association
For the Propagation of the Asian Carnation.
Have you ever been pregnant on Euston Station?

Dinner with the Dons of Saint Abysmas's College, Oxbridge

I am the spy from Ignorance
In my thundercloud gown I dine.
I am the Elephant Man who sits
Between Will Hay and Wittgenstein.

Who Goes Where?

Oh who is that man who wishes he'd stuck to the path
His suede shoes uncomfortably soaked in the dews of the lawn?
Oh that is the man with the face of a sad sardine
      And they call him Overdrawn.

Give It to Me Ghostly

give it to me ghostly
close-up and long-distance
i've an open policy
of misty non-resistance
so give it to me ghostly
shudder up and lisp a
bogey-woman promise
to your will o' the whisper

give it to me ghostly
spook it to me somehow
haunt me haunt me haunt me
oooo thanks i've come now

Bury My Bones with an Eddy Merckx

live people don't often
have eyes for the overhead stars
but gloom down roads
in micro-wave cars

they dunno how the rippling
of the wild air feels
frowning round town
in tombs on wheels

but ghosts ride bikes
free-wheeling mostly
singing songs like
Give It To Me Ghostly

ghosts got no rooty-tooty
duty to be done
cars are for bloody business
bikes for fun

Third Opinion

'Is he better off with it or without it?'
Said the doctor with the moustache.
Said the doctor with the beard:
'Well, frankly, Simon, I'm in two minds about it.'
They turned to the bed.
The patient had disappeared.

Money and Booze
(a love song)

He was as filthy as fivepence
And vacant as ginger-beer shandy
But she was as naughty as ninepence
And she went through his system like brandy

Social Being

'Come to the party! Isn't it time
You faced the world again?'
So I clenched my face and entered the place –
A roomful of boozing Mister Men.

Remember Red Lion Square?

I haven't heard any Moderates lately
Mention the name of Kevin Gateley,
The student who, so the Coroner said,
Died from 'a moderate blow to the head'.

The Christians Are Coming Goodbye Goodbye

They fought the good fight on six continents,
Cutting down the godless foe.
The Christians were Super-Campbells,
The whole world – their Glencoe.

Ode to Her

You so draggy Ms Maggie
The way you drag us down
The way you shake your finger
Way you frown your frown
But a day's soon dawning
When all the world will shout
We're gonna catch yer Ms Thatcher
You'll be dragged out

You so draggy Ms Maggie
You tore this land apart
With your smile like a laser
And your iceberg heart
You teach the old and jobless
What poverty means
You send the young men killing
The Irish and the Argentines

You so draggy Ms Maggie
With your million cuts
You slashed this country
Till it spilled its guts
You crucified parents
And their children too
Nailed 'em up by the million
Here's what we'll do

You so draggy Ms Maggie
Madonna of the Rich
We're gonna introduce you
On the Anfield pitch
Oh you can talk your meanest
But you as good as dead
When Yosser Hughes butts you
With his poor old head…

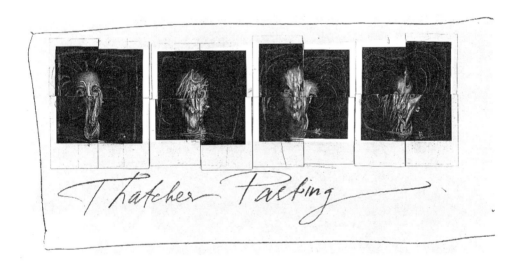

On the Beach at Cambridge

I am assistant to the Regional Commissioner
At Block E, Brooklands Avenue,
Communications Centre for Region 4,
Which used to be East Anglia.

I published several poems as a young man
But later found I could not meet my own high standards
So tore up all my poems and stopped writing.
(I stopped painting at eight and singing at five.)
I was seconded to Block E
From the Ministry for the Environment.

Since there are no established poets available
I have come out here in my MPC
(Maximum Protective Clothing)
To dictate some sort of poem or word-picture
Into a miniature cassette recorder.

When I first stepped out of Block E on to this beach
I could not record any words at all,
So I chewed two of the orange-flavoured pills
They give us for morale, switched on my Sony
And recorded this:
I am standing on the beach at Cambridge.
I can see a group in their MPC
Pushing Hoover-like and Ewbank-like machines
Through masses of black ashes.
The taller men are soldiers or police,
The others, scientific supervisors.
This group moves slowly across what seems
Like an endless car park with no cars at all.

I think that, in one moment,
All the books in Cambridge
Leapt off their shelves,
Spread their wings
And became white flames
And then black ash.
And I am standing on the beach at Cambridge.

You're a poet, said the Regional Commissioner,
Go out and describe that lot.

The University Library – a little hill of brick-dust.
King's College Chapel – a dune of stone-dust.
The sea is coming closer and closer.

The clouds are edged with green,
Sagging low under some terrible weight.
They move more rapidly than usual.

Some younger women with important jobs
Were admitted to Block E
But my wife was a teacher in her forties.
We talked it over
When the nature of the crisis became apparent.
We agreed somebody had to carry on.
That day I kissed her goodbye as I did every day
At the door of our house in Chesterton Road.
I kissed my son and my daughter goodbye.
I drove to Block E beside Hobson's Brook.
I felt like a piece of paper
Being torn in half.

And I am standing on the beach at Cambridge.
Some of the men in their MPC
Are sitting on the ground in the black ashes.
One is holding his head in both his hands.

I was forty-two three weeks ago.
My children painted me
Bright-coloured cards with poems for my birthday.
I stuck them with Blu-Tack on the kitchen door.
I can remember the colours.

But in one moment all the children in Cambridge
Spread their wings
And became white flames
And then black ash.

And the children of America, I suppose.
And the children of Russia, I suppose.

And I am standing on the beach at Cambridge
And I am watching the broad black ocean tide
Bearing on its shoulders its burden of black ashes.

And I am listening to the last words of the sea
As it beats its head against the dying land.

Religion, Royalty and the Arts

The Liberal Christ Gives a Press Conference

I would have walked on the water
But I wasn't fully insured.
And the BMA sent a writ my way
With the very first leper I cured.

I would've preached a golden sermon
But I didn't like the look of the Mount.
And I would've fed fifty thousand
But the Press wasn't there to count.

    And the businessmen in the temple
    Had a team of coppers on the door.
    And if I'd spent a year in the desert
    I'd have lost my pension for sure.

    I would've turned the water into wine
    But they weren't giving licences.
    And I would have died and been crucified
    But like – you know how it is.

    I'm going to shave off my beard
    And cut my hair,
    Buy myself some bulletproof
    Underwear
    I'm the Liberal Christ
    And I've got no blood to spare.

Many Many Many Mansions

*(An ode to the occasion of the completion of an interdenominational
Chaplaincy Centre at the University of Lancaster.)*

This house was built for God.
It looks good.

'You can sit on the toilet and cook your dinner, and you
don't have to stretch out at all,' a pregnant woman told us.

Another house for God,
In case he visits Lancaster University.

He had come home from work to find his flat flooded
with sewage overflowing from upstairs

Every new house for God
Is a joke by the rich against the poor

'If my baby lives, the welfare may give me a place
with two bedrooms. If it dies, I'll have to stay here.'

Every new house for God
Is blasphemy against humanity.

Christians and others, when you need to pray,
Go to the kitchens of the slums,
Kneel to the mothers of the slums,
Pray to the children of the slums.
The people of the slums will answer your prayers.

Miserable Sinners

Now I know that revolutionary Catholic priests have died fighting for freedom and socialism in South America, and Quaker schools are smashing, and Donald Soper's all right in his place, and some of the sayings of Jesus are worthy of William Blake – but to hell with organised religion.

In Ireland, the basic human needs of liberty, equality and fraternity go to blazes while the two big local superstitions fight it out.

If the professionals in the churches believe in Christ, why don't they work as he did? Jesus didn't take scholarships so he could study to become a rabbi. He didn't ask for a temple and a vicarage and a salary and a pension scheme. He didn't push for exclusive propaganda rights in schools.

To Jesus, the Churches of England and Rome would have been strictly science fiction. Vast, rich propaganda machines, thriving on spiritual blackmail.

He worked differently. He told as much of the truth as he could until they killed him – like many other good men, religious and irreligious. I've met many people like that, most of them members of no church, most of them completely unknown.

If the churches cared for this world, they would extract their hooks from their people, disestablish, disperse and house the people instead of God. De-escalate organised religion and some of the most hopeless political situations in the world would become clearer, even soluble. Even Ireland. Even the Middle East.

If you detect personal bitterness in the above, you are damn right. I will declare my interest. For a few years I attended a school where evangelism was the dominant religion. We used to go to camp in North Wales for intensive Bible readings and declarations of conversion.

The message sank in deep, and the message was guilt. And the punishment for guilt was Hell. I was taught the ugliness and vileness of the body. I was taught terror. The Hell we were threatened with was the Hell of the sermon in *Portrait of the Artist as a Young Man*.

In short, we were children with no defences, and we were violated by holy Hitchcocks. It took me about fifteen years to shake off most of that fear and disgust. I don't know what happened to the others.

Sure, this was an extreme case. Sure, it was way back in the nineteen-forties. But Frankenstein's monster (alias the Church of Christ) keeps rolling along, crushing children as it rolls.

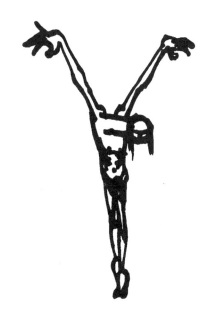

QUESTION: But what would you put in the place of organised religion?

ANSWER: Omnicreed.

QUESTION: What is Omnicreed?

ANSWER: A custom-built religion, which incorporates the most imaginative ideas of all religions and rejects the boring, terror-laden and anti-imaginative concepts.

QUESTION: Can you give me some examples?

ANSWER: You bet your sweet soul. The Anti-Imagination, known and rejected among Omnicreed initiates as The Brown Lump, embraces such concepts as the Sabbath, clergymen, popery, no popery and Cliff Richard in Westminster Abbey. On the other hand, Omnicreed awards its Good Church-keeping Certificate to such doctrines as The Immaculate Unction of Pope Joan, Nirvana as a Motel, the Bank of England Formation Dancing Team, Bulldozer Rallies, Calvin as the Inventor of Milk Chocolate, Nationalised Delicatessens, Zen Washing Lines and the Company of Dogs.

QUESTION: Have you got a light?

Sunday Poem

(to the Christians)

Eat this: God has a place,
Incense-deodorised, a vaulted mouth
Where the good dead always
Alleluia among towers of teeth.
Boring? In that honey of saliva?
They tell me male sharks come for seven
Or eight hours. Multiply forever –
You still can't count the heaven of Heaven.

Eat this: God has another place,
A gaol-hole. Walls contract and crush
Necks on to legs, bellies into faces
And all parts in a constipated hash
Of cancered madmen, vomiting and skinned,
Skewered in flames which rot, restore and rot,
Breathing only the tear-gas of their sins –
That's what the bad dead get.

Old Testament New Testament *or*
His Eye Is on the Blonde in the Third Row

Tugging at his zippers,
Sweat in waterfalls down his leathers,
God used to scream into the mike.
Blood-lightning spurted from the speakers
And the sparks were in his hair – yeah.

Then he decided to try for the family audience.

Quite Apart from the Holy Ghost

I remember God as an eccentric millionaire,
Locked in his workshop, beard a cloud of foggy-coloured hair,
Making the stones all different, each flower and disease,
Pulling the Laps in Lapland, making China for the Chinese,
Laying down the Lake of Lucerne as smooth as blue-grey lino,
Wearily inventing the appendix and the rhino,
Making the fine fur for the mink, fine women for the fur,
Man's brain a gun, his heart a bomb, his conscience – a blur.

Christ I can see much better from here,
And Christ upon the Cross is clear.
Jesus is stretched like the skin of a kite
Over the Cross, he seems in flight
Sometimes. At times it seems more true
That he is meat nailed up alive and pain all through.
But it's hard to see Christ for priests. That happens when
A poet engenders generations of advertising men.

The Eggs o' God

Last Thursday God manifested himself as a barrage balloon with varicose veins and descended on the Vatican. I'm shrivelling, he shouted to the Pope, once I was bigger than the Universe but now I'm shrinking fast. The bulk of God lolled in St Peter's Square, deflating soon to the size of a double-decker bus. Quick, cried God, before I vanish, one last request. When I've disappeared, put my eggs in a jar, keep in a cool place and run a world-wide search for a warm-hearted virgin. Let her hatch the eggs and then you'll find –

But by now God is a hissing football, and now he is a grapefruit, now a grape, and now the grape has exploded and nothing is left in the Square but the Eggs of God.

Four Switzers armed with money-trowels shovelled the golden spawn into a lucent white container and bore it to the Papal fridge.

At two in the morning a whisky cardinal staggered in, his stomach growling for a snack. Unfortunately he fancied caviar...

The Pope has risen frae his bed
On his twa holy legs
And doon the marble staircase gaed
Tae see the sacred eggs

O wha has stolen the Eggs o' God
Gae seek him near and far
O wha has stolen the Eggs o' God
Frae the Gentleman's Relish jar

Then up and spak the Cardinal
His voice was like a Boeing
O I hae eaten the Eggs o' God
And I'm eight miles tall, and growing...

A Leaflet to Be Dropped on China

(This is a translation back into English of a dialogue between two ordinary Britons. This dialogue is to be printed as the first in a series of leaflets to be dropped on China in order to explain about Western Civilisation.)

BILL: I say, Fred, what do you think about Her Majesty The Queen?

FRED: Well, Bill, I am bound to say that I do not envy Her Her job!

BILL: What? But surely Her life must be both enjoyable and rewarding. With those dogs and pearls and soldiers and things.

FRED: Would you say so, Bill? But Her Majesty has many onerous duties to perform. Is not Her motto, I Serve?

BILL: No Fred, I think it is God Save the Queen. I saw a film starring Her on television. She was waving to a group of policemen who were guarding a patch of snow.

FRED: Be that as it may, Bill. She is expected to lend Her name to charities of every sort, to attend with the horse racing and to shake hands among other things with members of the Family of Commonwealth without regard for race, colour, creed or money.

BILL: Well, Fred, when you put it like that old comrade, I suppose Her average day must be a full and demanding one! But surely She is well paid for Her efforts!

FRED: Aha Bill, you have fallen into a common fallacy. Her Majesty the Queen is by no means well paid considering! The income from Her own estates provides the wherewithal for Her everyday expenses like ice creams, er and pearls!!

BILL: Well, well, that is surprising!

FRED: And on top of that to boot, She is also Chief of the Church of England!!!

BILL: Good heavens, Fred! I would not like to work as hard! I would not like to be the Queen for all the tea in China!!

FRED: No more, Bill, would I!!!!

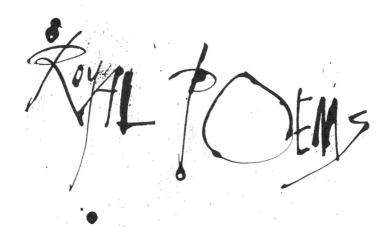

ROYAL BLOOD

Another Prince Is Born

Fire off the bells, ring out wild guns,
Switch on the sun for the son of sons.
For loyal rubbernecks who wait
Stick a notice on the gate.
Thrill to frill and furbelow,
God Save Sister Helen Rowe.
Lord Evans, Peel, Hall and Sir John
Guard the cot he dribbles on.
An angel in a Hunter jet
Circles round his bassinet.
Inform *The Times, Debrett, Who's Who*,
Better wake C. Day Lewis too.

Comes the parade of peers and peasants,
The Queen bears children, they bear presents –
Balls and toy guardsmen, well-trained parrots,
A regal rattle (eighteen carats),
And one wise man with myrrh-oiled hair
Brings a six-foot teddy bear
From the Birmingham Toy Fair.

Lying in State

He's dead. Into the vault and out
Shuffles the reverent conga.
With his intestines taken out
He will stay sweeter longer.

Poem on the Occasion of the Return of
Her Majesty the Queen from Canada

Some love Jesus and some love brandy
Some love Schweitzer or the boys in blue
Some love squeezing that Handy Andy
But I love model airplane glue
   Gloucester Gladiator
   Super-Constellation
   U2 U2 U2
I can see all of Russia from up here

Once upon a time I couldn't leave the ground
My wings were warping and my props were through
No elastic could turn them round
Till I found model airplane glue
   Supermarine Spitfire
   Vickers Viscount
   Junkers Junkie
Come fly with me

Take one sniff and my engines start
Second sniff I'm Blériot and Bader too
Holds me together when I'm flying apart
So I love model airplane glue
   BOAC
   El-Al
   Sputnik
I am Eagle I am Eagle

Some love a copper and some love a preacher
Some love Hiroshima and Waterloo
Some love the Beatles and some love Nietzsche
But I love model airplane glue
   A bit of wire
   A rubber band
   Balsa wood
   That's man
And a man needs glue.

Royal Poems

The Daily Telegraph *wrote asking me: 'Could you, for instance, let us have some verse on how you see the relationship that exists between the Prince of Wales and the Welsh people? Obviously it is quite impossible for us to let you have a clear brief, but what we hope to achieve is something that will in some way reflect the Welsh mood as we see it, or even as they see it.' I responded by return of post with the following:*

To Charles Windsor-Mountbatten

Royalty is a neurosis.
Get well soon.

The Daily Telegraph *rejected my contribution politely, but they'd started something and, after a week's research in which I established beyond reasonable doubt my claim to the throne of England, I wrote a series of regal bits in my new persona as the Rightful King of England.*

Loyal Ode to Myself on My Installation as Prince of Yorkshire

Applauded by the loyal West Riding drizzle
I progressed up the A65
Bearing the symbol of my temporal power,
An iced lolly, very cold and powerfully purple.
Under my purple breath
I swore eternal fealty to myself
Against all manner of folks.
Nobody threw any eggs at ME.

Decree to All Members of the Church of England

We, His Majesty, the Rightful King of England,
Do hereby publish and decree
And do most hideously command on pain of pain
That all baptised members of our Church of England
Shall sell all that they have
And bring the wherewithal therefrom
To our most Royal Treasury.
We shall await your loyal tributes
At the summit of Primrose Hill
At noon on October 24th this year,
Cash please, no cheques.
Yours sincerely,
Defender of the Faith.

The Royal Prerogative of Mercy

Put that woman down at once!
We know she's upset you,
We know she's got a face
Like a breach of the peace,
But give her back her horse,
Return her knickers.
We are a merciful King
Even to women in military uniform
Who pretend to be the Queen of England.

The Prince of Wailers

Edward the Eighth
crazy king
He knew how to shake that thing.

Royal Whodunnit

after the Coronation
they found upon the Throne
a new-laid turd
as hard as stone

My Shy Di in Newspaperland

*(All the lines are quoted from the British Press on Royal Engagement day,
the only slight distortions appear in the repeats of the four-line chorus.
Written in collaboration with Alistair Mitchell.)*

Who will sit where in the forest of tiaras?
She is an English rose without a thorn.
Love is in their stars, says Susie.
She has been plunged headfirst into a vast goldfish bowl.

Did she ponder as she strolled for an hour through Belgravia?
Will they, won't they? Why, yes they will.
They said so yesterday.
He said: 'Will you?'
She said: 'Yes.'
So did his mother – and so say all of us.

Who will sit where in the head of the goldfish?
She is an English forest without a tiara.
Love is in their roses, says Thorny.
She has been plunged starsfirst into a vast susie bowl.

Most of the stories in this issue were written
By James Whitaker, the *Daily Star* man
Who has always known that Diana and Prince Charles would marry.
He watched them fishing on the River Dee –
And Lady Diana was watching him too.
She was standing behind a tree using a mirror
To watch James Whitaker at his post,
James Whitaker, the man who always knew.

Who will sit where in the stars of Susie?
She is an English head without a goldfish.
Love is in their forests, says Tiara.
She has been plunged rosefirst into a vast thorn bowl.

All about Di.
Shy Di smiled and blushed.
Lady Di has her eyelashes dyed.
My shy Di.

She descends five times from Charles II –
Four times on the wrong side of the blanket
And once on the right side.

Who will sit where in the rose of thorns?
She is an English star without a susie.
Love is in their heads, says Goldfish.
She has been plunged forestfirst into a vast tiara bowl.

Flatmate Carolyn Pride was in the loo
When she heard of the engagement.
'Lady Diana told me through the door,' she said last night.
'I just burst into tears. There were floods and floods of tears.'

Who will sit where in the forest of tiaras?
She is an English rose without a thorn.
Love is in their stars, says Susie.
She has been plunged headfirst into a vast goldfish bowl.

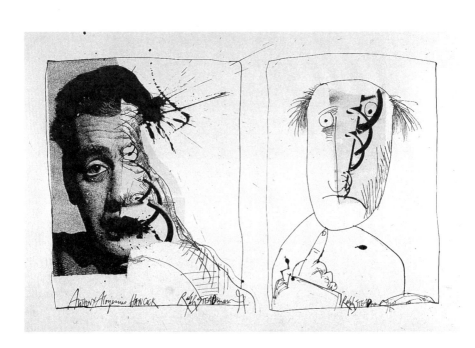

Goodbye

He breathed in air, he breathed out light.
Charlie Parker was my delight.

Jimmy Giuffre Plays 'The Easy Way'

A man plodding through blue-grass fields.
He's here to decide whether the grass needs mowing.
He sits on a mound and taps his feet on the deep earth.
He decides the grass doesn't need mowing for a while.

Buddy Bolden

He bust through New Orleans
On his cornet night and day,
Buddy kept on stompin'
Till he was put away.

He chose his girls like kings do
And drank like earth was hell,
But when they tried to cut him
He played like Gabriel.

The notes shot out his cornet
Like gobs come off a ship.
You felt the air get tighter
And then you heard it rip.

They threw him in the bughouse
And took away his horn.
He hadn't felt so mean since
The day that he was born.

Some say corn liquor done it
Or layin' a bad whore
But I guess he blew so much out
He couldn't think no more.

Bessie Smith in Yorkshire

As I looked over the billowing West Riding
A giant golden tractor tumbled over the horizon
The grass grew blue and the limestone turned to meat
For Bessie Smith was bumping in the driver's seat.

Threw myself down on the fertilised ground and cried:
'When I was a foetus I loved you, and I love you now you've died.'
She was bleeding beauty from her wounds in the Lands of Wrong
But she kept on travelling and she spent all her breathing on song.

I was malleted into the earth as tight as a gate-post
She carried so much life I felt like the ghost of a ghost
She's the river that runs straight uphill
Hers is the voice brings my brain to a standstill

Black tracking wheels
Roll around the planet
Seeds of the blues
Bust through the concrete

My pale feet fumble along
The footpaths of her midnight empire

The Great Bell in Paul Robeson's Chest

the great bell   speaks
the great bell   cast in blood
the great bell   speaks

the great bell   over the sea
the great bell   through the air
the great bell   across the land

the great bell   speaks

the great bell   freedom
the great bell   equality
the great bell   brotherhood

the great bell   speaks

the great bell   now
                            now
                            now

the great bell   speaks

the great bell   weeping
                            thinking
                            laughing
                            dreaming

the great bell   loving

the great bell   speaks
the great bell   cast in blood
the great bell   speaks

What to Do if You Meet Nijinsky

The special child
Remains a child
Knowing that everything else
Is smaller, meaner and less gentle.

Watch the creature standing
Like a fountain in a photograph.
He's moving carefully as a leaf
Growing in a hothouse.
What are the roots?
What is the stem?
What are the flowers?
Nijinsky
Dancing too much truth.

If you don't kill Nijinsky
He's going to turn you into Nijinsky.
You'll live like a leaf, die like a leaf,
Like Nijinsky.

Sweet magical
Skinned
Alive
Animal

You must decide for yourself how you're going to kill Nijinsky.

Leave him in the prison
Whose stones are cut so cleverly
They fit every contour of his skin exactly.

Leave him collapsing
In the foreign forest clearing
While the pine trees burn around him like a circle of matches.
Climb into your car and drive like a rocket right out of the world of feeling.

Leave Nijinsky dancing
The dance of lying very still

Most People...

Most people ignore poetry
because
most poetry ignores people

To the Statues in Poets' Corner, Westminster Abbey

You stony bunch of pockskinned whiteys,
Why kip in here? Who sentenced you?
They are buying postcards of you,
The girls in safety knickers.
Tombfaces, glumbums,
Wine should be jumping out all of your holes,
You should have eyes that roll, arms that knock things over,
Legs that falter and working cocks.
Listen.
On William Blake's birthday we're going to free you,
Blast you off your platforms with a blowtorch full of brandy
And then we'll all stomp over to the Houses of Parliament
And drive them into the Thames with our bananas.

Banana

a phallus going round a corner

carefully

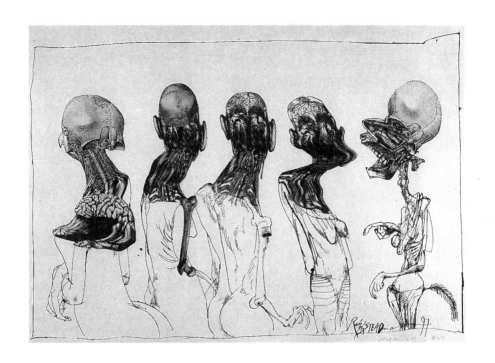

Crusoe Dying in England

Always the seagulls cry on me
Weak from the waves. They tell me tales,
Say: Now you breathe the English sky;
You have been rescued from the toils
Of the black island. All the day
They speak fair times. But constantly
Caged in my chest a huge fowl wails
And screams the truth above the lie:
England is drowned. Old age despoils
My senses. I am cast away.

My body is a breathing weight
Obscenely formed to be my shame.
I cannot show it to the light
But hide it in my hollow room;
For now the rooted traps are set,
The springs are sour and my estate
Is lost to me. I have no name.
Thick grow the poison weeds, no flight
Is possible. The branches loom
Shining above with lazy sweat.

Fruit hangs and drops upon the hut
Endlessly from heavy trees.
I have no will to hook or net
Fantastic fish I used to prize.
Shuddering skies melt in the heat
To soak my limbs. My heart is shut
And locked to hope. My silly knees
Kissing the earth, let me forget
The ghosts who turn before my eyes,
Companions of sea and street.

We would go, swaggering and fine,
To rake the taverns of a port.
My storming friends, we loved in vain
For now your eyes are all put out.
Shackled along the rusty chains
Of thought, you are not truly mine.
Captives, but you will not be taught
To sing, or move, or speak again.
Bad air invades me from without
My friends lie sullen in my brains.

Crusoe? I am some other thing,
A city caught in evil days
Of plague and fire: I am a throng
Of shaking men: I am a race
Undone by fear, for I was born
In a cursed country. Who is King?
Who is the ruler of this shattered place
Myself? The Bible God? But strong
Crusoe is dead. I have no face;
An old mad god, my powers gone.

Whitman on Wheels

Fanfare: in transports over transport
I salute all passenger-carrying machines –
The admirable automobile, the glottal motor-cycle,
The womby capsule bound for Mars.
The tube train (see how well it fits its tube).
The vibrant diesel, the little engine that could

And all manner of airplanes whether they carry
Hostesses, hogs or horror.
Gargantuan traction engines.
Curmudgeonly diggers, bulldozers, dinosauric tank-tracked cranes.
Zoomers, splutterers, purrers and gliders
I salute you all,
And also the reliable tricycle.

Canine Canto

Dogs thurber through the whitman grass
On wild shakespearean excursions.
They have no waugh or corneille class
In their laurence sterne diversions.
They sniff blake blooms and patchen weeds,
They have no time for strindberg doom,
Or walks on firm jane austen leads,
Formal pope gardens or the baudelaire room.
As for donne love, while going it,
They lawrence without knowing it.

Thank You Dick Gregory

King Lear kept shouting at his Fool:
'These children squeeze, bruise and knot my arteries.
I ache and shake with fatherhood.
Sex can't ache or shake me now
But bawdiness makes my old eyes shine.
So make me jokes that jump, and tumble,
A whole crowd of jokes, a courtful of pretty people jokes
So I can meet each one just once
And then forget, meeting another joke.'
But the Fool made a face like an expensive specialist,
He put one hand on the king's pulse, one on his own heart
And said: 'Your Majesty, you're dying, man.'

Dick Gregory, the funny man, left the glad clapping hands
Of San Francisco, where tigers still survive,
To walk in the dust of Greenwood, Mississippi.
He walked as Gary Cooper used to walk
In Westerns, but Gregory walked blackly, seriously, not pretending.
He burned as Brando burns in movies
But the flames behind his eyes were black
And everything his eyes touched scorched.
His jokes crackled in the air,
Gags like Bob Hope's, but these were armed and black.
Liberals realised that they were dwarfs,
Colonels got blisters, and Gregory laughed.

114

When Dick Gregory reached the South
They told him his two-month son was dead.
I heard that today.
I had to write and say:
Thank you Dick Gregory,
I send as much love as you will take from me,
My blackest and my whitest love.
King Lear is dying of your jokes,
Of your flames, of your tall walking –
Thank you Dick Gregory.

Lullaby for William Blake

Blakehead, babyhead,
Your head is full of light.
You sucked the sun like a gobstopper.
Blakehead, babyhead,
High as a satellite on sunflower seeds,
First man-powered man to fly the Atlantic,
Inventor of the poem which kills itself.
The poem which gives birth to itself,
The human form, jazz, Jerusalem
And other luminous, luminous galaxies.
You out-spat your enemies.
You irradiated your friends.
Always naked, you shaven, shaking tyger-lamb,
Moon-man, moon-clown, moon-singer, moon-drinker,
You never killed anyone.
Blakehead, babyhead,
Accept this mug of crude red wine –
I love you.

Birthday Song for Spike Hawkins, the Unholy Ghost

She rubbed me in the pub
She rubbed me in the pub
She rubbed me in the pub
NO SINGING ALLOWED!

Love For Tony

Tony Jackson is a walking jungle.
Tony Jackson can cry.
Tony Jackson, when elected, will encourage breasts.
Tony Jackson will lend you his invisible roller-skates.
Tony Jackson bawls back at you, balls back at you.
Tony Jackson sweats the blues.
Tony Jackson can't give you anything but love, baby.
Tony Jackson is alight.
Tony Jackson, when elected, will encourage jungle.
Tony Jackson is a walking ball.
Tony Jackson can't give you anything but blue sweat, baby.
Tony Jackson will lend you breasts.
Tony Jackson sweats roller-skates.
Tony Jackson, when elected, will cry.

For David Mercer

I like dancers who stamp.
Elegance
Is for certain trees, some birds,
Expensive duchesses, expensive whores,
Elegance, it's a small thing
Useful to minor poets and minor footballers.
But big dancers, they stamp and they stamp fast,
Trying to keep their balance on the globe.
Stamp, to make sure the earth's still there,
Stamp, so the earth knows that they're dancing.
Oh the music puffs and bangs along beside them
And the dancers sweat, they like sweating
As the lovely drops slide down their scarlet skin
Or shake off into the air
Like notes of music.
I like dancers, like you, who sweat and stamp
And crack the ceiling when they jump.

116

U–S–S–R Spells Happy

JOLLY OLD, JOLLY OLD DOSTOEVSKY,
JOLLY OLD, JOLLY OLD DOSTOEVSKY,
JOLLY OLD, JOLLY OLD DOSTOEVSKY,
HE WENT TO THE TALKIES
With the Gorkies.

Hear the Voice of the Critic

There are too many colours.
The Union Jack's all right, selective,
Two basic colours and one negative,
Reasonable, avoids confusion.
   (Of course I respect the red, white and blue)

But there are too many colours.
The rainbow, well it's gaudy, but I am
Bound to admit, a useful diagram
When treated as an optical illusion.
   (Now I'm not saying anything against rainbows)

But there are too many colours.
Take the sea. Unclassifiable.
The sky – the worst offender of all,
Tasteless as Shakespeare, especially at sunset.
   (I wish my body were all one colour).

There are too many colours.
I collect flat white plates.
You ought to see my flat white plates.
In my flat white flat I have a perfect set,
   (It takes up seven rooms).

There are too many colours.

The Ballad of the Death of Aeschylus

Eagle flying along
hey hey
Eagle flying along
Swinging his golden all along the hey hey sky

Tortoise rumbling along
hey hey
Tortoise rumbling along
Dreaming of salad if you want the hey hey truth

But that was one heap of an
Astigmatic eagle
Astigmatic eagle
The kind of person
Who looks at a tortoise
And believes he's seeing casserole

Eagle swivelling down
hey hey
Eagle swivelling down
Clamping that tortoise into his beak
Dragging him up into a neighbouring cloud
And shutting the hey hey door

   Aeschylus was steaming through Athens
   Somewhere near the Parthenon Gents
   It is believed
   Aeschylus was steaming through Athens
   Out to get his tragical propens-
   ities relieved

That's the hey hey set up so remember it love
Man down below and an eagle plus a tortoise up above
Better carve that message in a durable cheese
And let it learn you a bit of manners please

It wasn't one of your charter flights
The eagle got Aeschylus in his sights

It was tortoise away and super-zap
Doing kerflumph and possibly BAP
Does anyone want a flat-headed tragedian?

Poor old bloody Aeschylus
hey hey
Poor old bloody Aeschylus
Come to that poor old bloody tortoise

A Good Idea

It should be the kind which stiffens and grows a skin
But the creamier kind will do.
Anyway, the Royal Albert Hall must be filled with custard.

Gaston the Peasant

Gaston liked being a peasant. He enjoyed all the things which peasants usually like, elemental things like being born, living and, something he looked forward to with oafish optimism, dying. Often, seated on a sack of blackened truffles in the steam of the peat fire, he would speak of these things:

'We peasants are almost excessively privileged,' he would vouch, in the expressive dialect of the Basques, 'in that not only do we delight in the elemental joys of Mankind, but also in that we are denied the manifold responsibilities accorded will-he nill-he to the holder of high office.'

Gaston had lived a long time, seen much, known many, done little. He was sketched eating turnips by Van Gogh. D.H. Lawrence dropped in to talk to him about the blood. He once tried to cheer up Emile Zola. Orwell slept with his pigs for the experience. Ernest Hemingway borrowed his pitchfork He did not return. He did not return the pitchfork.

Lady Macbeth in the Saloon Bar Afterwards

It was all going surprisingly well –
Our first school matinee and we'd got up to
My sleepwalking scene with the minimum of titters...
Right, enter me, somnambulistically.
One deep sigh. Then some lout tosses
A banana on to the fore-stage.
It got a round? Darling, it got a thunderstorm!
Of course, we carried on, but suddenly
We had a panto audience
Yelling out: 'Look out! He's behind you!'
Murders, battles, Birnham Wood, great poetry –
All reduced to mockery.
The Bard upstaged by a banana.
Afterwards we had a flaming row in the Grenville
About just who should have removed it
And just when –
One of the servants, obviously.

And ever since, at every performance:
Enter myself in those exquisite ribbons
And – plomp – a new out-front banana.
Well, yes, it does affect all our performances
But actually, they seem to love it.
And how, now Ben's in Canada
Doling out Wesker to the Eskimos,
Can we decide who exits with banana?
You can't expect me to parade down here,
Do a sort of boob-baring curtsey and announce:
'Is this a banana that I see before me?'
Anyway, darling, we may have egg on our faces –
But we've got a hit on our hands.

Two Paintings by Manuel Mendive

1. The road is a snake guarded by vultures
   A man on white crutches
   hauls a wagonload of corpses.
   He is crying blood.

2. God sits creating a bright halo of birds.
   He sits on a mountain of dark people
   who are impaled by everyday nails.

To the Organisers of a Poetry Reading by Hugh MacDiarmid

You chose the wrong place –
A neutral room with tawny blinds pulled down.
You pulled the wrong audience –
The gabbiest cultural bureaucrats in town.
You picked the wrong poet –
Too clever too daft too great for you to deserve his spittle

And you brought the wrong whisky
And you only bought him half a bottle.

Private Transport

round and round
his private roundabout
drives the little critic's car –
a sneer on four square wheels

What the Mermaid Told Me
(for the Fiftieth Anniversary of the British Broadcasting Corporation.)

Every sentence in the middle section of the piece was broadcast
by BBC TV during the period 13 July – 12 August 1972.

Strapped on my aqualung and flippered my way
To the bed of the electric ocean.
The water was flickering white and grey
And thick as calamine lotion.
Groped along the rocks till my hand came to rest
On the luke-warm pudding of a mermaid's breast.
She was British, broad, corporate and fiftyish
With a hint of aristocracy
Her top was woman and her arse was fish
And this is what she said to me:

   'How dangerous are these cable cars?
   We have a lot of fun on this show.
   When is all this killing going to stop?
   I think they deserve some applause, don't you?

   'We are very environment-conscious
   This is like a bloody Xmas grotto.
   What if everyone else refused to obey
   The laws of which they don't approve?

   'What does Muswell Hill mean to you?
   Will the ceasefire stick?
   He was not the man to embarrass the police.
   I think they deserve some applause, don't you?

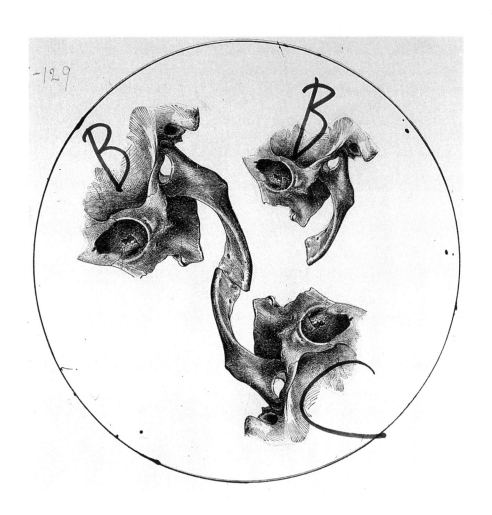

'I came to an arrangement with him
To come up with 40 million dollars.
When I sing my songs you can't sit still,
Your big toe shoot up in your boot.

'If only women could get on with women
Like men get on with men.
It's lovely for me to be sitting
In a seat like this again

'Just in one day our lives were crushed.
I don't want to be an old curmudgeon.
Are the five senses enough any more?
I think they deserve some applause, don't you?

'You're doing to this country what Hitler failed to do.
Has he been the victim of a personal witch-hunt?
He makes no bones about carrying the can
For Rio Tinto Zinc.

'There is going to be a very high attrition rate
In this field of 26 starters,
Look all around, there's nothing but blue skies.
We'll kill 'em all or get back into Cambodia.

'I've had people who've had conversion experiences
Following leucotomy.
You can never be certain of anything in Ireland.
I think they deserve some applause, don't you?

'British public life is singularly free from any taint of corruption at all.
Our towns are almost ready to be destroyed, they are uninhabitable,
They are completely contrary to human life
The British found it necessary to intervene to protect their interests.
There are so few young women in Highbury who are in any way suitable
What has become of your traditional British phlegm and common sense?
We're only giving the public what they want.
I think they deserve some applause, don't you?'

The mermaid was ten thousand times as heavy as me
And the scales of her tail were moulting.
But since she was the hottest thing in the sea
She was also the least revolting.
I proposed a little sexual action
And she smiled (which was mostly gaps),
And she wriggled her satisfaction
As she whispered to me: 'Perhaps.'

Discovery

Unpopular, Tibetan and four foot two,
He ran an underground cocktail bar
Near the pit-face of a Congolese coal-mine.
Nobody would listen to his stories
So he scribbled them on the backs of beer-mats,
One sentence on each mat.
Because he hated coal
He wrote, mostly, about the sea.

Years later two critics from Cambridge
Spent their honeymoon at the same colliery.
They discovered a black chamber
Empty but for a hundred thousand beer-mats.

After years of beer-mat shuffling and transcription
The critics published the text
As The Fictional Works of Joseph Conrad.
Three cheers for the critics!
Three cheers for Cambridge!
Where would Joseph Conrad be without them?
Down the mine.

Where be Joseph Conrad?
Two hundred yards down in the same Congolese pit,
Serving mint juleps to the husky miners,
Speaking when he is spoken to.

There Are Not Enough of Us

How much verse is magnificent?
Point oh oh oh oh one per cent.
How much poetry is second-rate?
Around point oh oh oh oh eight.
How much verse is a botched hotch potch?
Ninety-eight per cent by my watch.
How much poetry simply bores?
None of mine and all of yours.

There Are Too Many of Them

Most poets are bad poets, the poor creatures.
Much worse than that: most teachers are bad teachers.

Improvisation Time in the Rehearsal Room

today, says the director, i want you to be
absolutely, totally free.

actors begin to loosen up as they've always done before.
how long, says the tough actress, are we allowed to be free for?
for as long as you like, darling. she picks up her mac,
walks out the door and never comes back.

the hot drinks machine
sounds like a guillotine.

Oscar Wilde in Flight

motherofpearlcoloured feathers
preposterous wingspan
glides over earthscapes waterscapes icescapes
dropping a trail of surprise green blossoms

and archangel Oscar
rolls with laughter as he dives
through the sunset revolving door
of a cloud decked out like the Café Royal

only once in every thousand years
he downs a glass of liquid granite
and privately weeps with memory
for the butchers chopped his wings to stumps
and threw him into Reading Gaol
with the other amputees
he weeps for them
not for himself
then he shakes away his tears

and up he soars again
swinging his way
throughout the blue and white in happy flight

For Basil Bunting

There was a Northumbrian spuggie*
Who sang when the weather was muggy
    When they said: 'It's not spring'
    He continued to sing
Like a stubborn Northumbrian spuggie.

* *spuggie*: sparrow

129

John Keats Eats His Porridge

It was hot enough to blister
The red paint of his mouth.
But if he let it lie there, glistening,
then clipped segments from the circumference,
it slid down like a soggy bobsleigh.

Grey as November, united as the kingdom,
but the longer he stared into that dish of porridge
the more clearly he traced
under the molten sugar
the outline of each flake of oatmeal...

When the milk made its slow blue-tinted leap from jug to bowl
the porridge became an island.
John's spoon vibrated in his hand.
The island became a planet.
He made continents, he made seas.

This is strange porridge.
Eat it all up.

A Blessing for Kenneth Patchen's Grave

may hummingbirds
forever hover over
white and purple domes of clover

Roger McGough the Travel Courier

Roger just drove us in his wonderbus
Over prairies of funny wheat
And down a dinosaur burrow.

We piled out into the big dark.

A pause, made by his eyes.

And then his word-touch lit upon,
One by one,
The slow-growing
Stalactites and stalagmites
Of the saddest cavern of his heart.

So why are you questioning him
About the design of Austrian gravy-boats?

*A Gublisher Is an Expensive Indian Settee Made of Dark Red Suede Inlaid With Gold

The writer
Sits at his typewriter.
His mind is drear and his eyes are blear
As he thinks: Oh Dear, Oh Dear

The writer
Taps on his typewriter.
These words appear
In grey on white: Oh Dear, Oh Dear

The publisher
Curled up on his gublisher
Remarks: 'It ain't King Lear'
As he reads: 'Oh Dear, Oh Dear.'

The publisher
Switches on his electric Rubbslisher
And shoves in the sincere
Author of 'Oh Dear, Oh Dear'.

The Brave Emergency Poet

'Poets and doctors are allowed to double-park in Paris –
but only in an emergency…'
    YASMINA NOURRIS

A distraught femme leans from a window in the Rue des Poissons de Merde, Paris, France. 'Come queek!', elle vouchsafes, 'My 'orseband, 'e is strucken weez ze Prose dreadé! Un Poète! un Poète!'

A street-urchin (Piaf) levers a cobble from the rue, takes aim and smashes the stained-glass face of the Poetry Alarm.

Somewhere on the Left Bank a huge golden bell chimes in the attic of an Emergency Troubadour. Hugging his mistresses au revoir, he leaps for the greased silver birch which grows up through a hole in his floor, slides down it, unharnesses a white horse with unpretentious wings and leap imaginatively into the butter-soft saddle.

Meanwhile, in the Rue des Poissons de Merde, the unimaginary invalid is convulsed by great and small shocks of heart-numbing prose –

'As it were! As it happened! Far be it from me!', he exclaims, boring his own soul to tears. 'He knocked at the door, and, without waiting for a reply, he entered,' screams the pauvre. 'The club to which I have the honour to belong has its premises behind the Cathedral!', he shrieks, as the virus of prose devours more and more of his visionary corpuscles.

Leaving his feathered steed DOUBLE-PARKED, the Urgency Poet stands at the sick-bedside, ripping open the zip of his Bardic Bag. Swiftly he applies a compress of jellied gloves and cog-wheels. He shampoos the agoniser with the foam of nettles. He dances obliquely with a sad measuring-dog. And of course he chants lamp-post litanies, carves sonnets upon bars of soap, splashes the sheets with verses of vivid violet and conducts a blues band of favourite dolphins.

Slowly the mortified prosee begins to be stirred, like a novitiate mayonnaise. His flesh begins to crawl with happiness. Click goeth his neck and suddenly all the prose founts out of his lard like goodbye pus…

Back in his garret once more, the Lone Laureate hangs up his Orphic Underwear. 'Another day, another dolour,' murmurs the Randy Rhymester as he wends his gee-whizz way from bed to bed to bed to bed to bed.

Tribute to Monsieur Verne

Jules
Rules

First Tribute To Mark Twain

On the Mississippi's brim
I rode the raft with Huck and Jim

Second Tribute to Mark Twain

Don't be daft
Go by raft

To a Lady

Is she a trouble maker?
She wouldn't lower herself to be;
But she owns fifty-one per cent of the shares
In a shit-stirring factory.

Ring of Dirty Water

I'm a rotter
I shot a
otter

Common Bloody Market Poem

a shroud rustles –
i remember brussels

Forster the Flying Fish

Forster the Flying Fish
In a purple tank did dwell.
I say dwell, it sounds damper than 'lived'
And also I would be the first to inform you
Were Forster the Flying Fish to be dead.
And 'did dwell' gives a quirky kind of antiquated
Twist of the wrist to the opening lines,
Good.
I mean the bones of this poem to show
And I make no bones about it.

Forster was named Forster by his master
After the liberal novelist.
Forster the Flying Fish was born to stunt,
At least he thought of himself as a stunt fish
But he never learned the knack of stunting.

Look, I promise you the critics will hate this poem.
They hate all poems they haven't read already.
However, the audience of gentle, wealthy readers
Who drooled over Tarka the Otter, Hazel the Bunny,
Jonathan Livingstone Vulture,
Bebop the Hobbit and Dolly the Wet Hen –
Surely they will salute
Forster the Flying Fish,
The latest Literary animal hero.

Forster the Flying Fish
Had a sidekick –
A slick amphibian called Cissy the Coelacanth.
Together they paddled and lapped round the globe,
Righting the wrongs of the animal kingdom –
Forster taking care of war in the air,
Cissy looking after land jobs.

If you have intelligent pets
Ask them to complete this poem.
I've got stomach ache.

The Oxford Hysteria of English Poetry

Back in the caveman days business was fair.
Used to turn up at Wookey Hole,
Plenty of action down the Hole
Nights when it wasn't raided.
They'd see my bear-gut harp
And the mess at the back of my eyes
And 'Right,' they'd say, 'make poetry.'
So I'd slam away at the three basic chords
And go into the act –
A story about the sabre-toothed tigers with a comic hero,
A sexy one with an anti-wife clubbing twist –
Good progressive stuff mainly,
Get ready for the Bronze Age, all that.
And soon it would be 'Bring out the woad!'
Yeah, woad. We used to get high on woad.

The Vikings only wanted sagas
Full of gigantic deadheads cutting off each other's vitals
Or Beowulf Versus the Bog People.
The Romans weren't much better
Under all that armour you could tell they were soft
With their central heating
And poets with names like Horace.

Under the Normans the language began to clear
Became a pleasure to write in,
Yes, write in, by now everyone was starting
To write down poems.
Well, it saved memorising and improvising
And the peasants couldn't get hold of it.
Soon there were hundreds of us
Most of us writing under the name
Of Geoffrey Chaucer.
Then suddenly we were knee-deep in sonnets.
Holinshed ran a headline:
BONANZA FOR BARDS.

It got fantastic –
Looning around from the bear-pit to the Globe,
All those freak-outs down the Mermaid,
Kit Marlowe coming on like Richard the Two,
A virgin Queen in a ginger wig
And English poetry in full whatsit –
Bloody fantastic, but I never found any time
To do any writing till Willy finally flipped –
Smoking too much of the special stuff
Sir Walter Raleigh was pushing.

Cromwell's time I spent on cultural committees.

Then Charles the Second swung down from the trees
And it was sexual medley time
And the only verses they wanted
Were epigrams on Chloe's breasts
But I only got published on the back of her left knee-cap.

Next came Pope and Dryden
So I went underground.
Don't mess with the Mafia.

Then suddenly – WOOMF –
It was the Ro-man-tic Re-viv-al
And it didn't matter how you wrote,
All the public wanted was a hairy great image.
Before they'd even print you
You had to smoke opium, die of consumption,
Fall in love with your sister
And drown in the Mediterranean (not at Brighton).
My publisher said: 'I'll have to remainder you
Unless you go and live in a lake or something
Like this bloke Wordsworth.'

After that there were about
A thousand years of Tennyson
Who got so bored with himself
That he changed his name
To Kipling at half-time.
Strange that Tennyson should be
Remembered for his poems really,
We always thought of him
As a golfer.

There hasn't been much time
For poetry since the Twenties

What with leaving the Communist Church
To join the Catholic Party
And explaining why in the *CIA Monthly*.
In 1963, for one night only,
I became the fourth Liverpool Marx Brother.
There was Groucho McGough,
Chico Henri, Harpo Patten
And me, I was Zeppo,
Yer, I was Pete Best.
Finally I was given the Chair of Comparative Ambiguity
At Armpit University, Java.
It didn't keep me busy,
But it kept me quiet.
It seemed like poetry had been safely tucked up for the night.

The Uncollected Works of Volcano Jones

What I Did in the Silver Jubilee

Every time I felt like smiling
I went indoors so nobody could see I wasn't in pain
Every time I felt like farting
I went to church or up in a plane

What I Think of Some of My Rivals

Walt Whitman was a bit much
John Betjeman was a bit little
John Keats was bit by a virus
Pablo Neruda was a bit off the map
Jomo Kenyatta turned out better than expected
Kick pillarboxes if you like pain
My grandmother always used to say there are millions of batty people
She used to say Gentlemen Lift The Seat
She used to say Leave Yourself Alone

There Is a Green Hill Right on Top of Us

I brought up all my hate
And arranged it on a plate
And served it up for dinner
To the fucking State

On the Composer Who Wrote 'God Save the Noble Czar'

In 1789
Was born Alexis Lwoff
In 1870
He buggered off

What about the National Theatre Then?

Bid the bells ring
Ken Campbell is King
Nick some gongs and bang 'em
The Pope is Chris Langham

They are the Red Devils of the free-fall intellect
And their writing is more like what you might expect
From mid-air jungle monkeys than from any human
That's why they deserve the love of every good man and woman

The Chanteuse and the Obsolete Beast

Dinah Shore saw a dinosaur
Dinah Shore saw a dinosaur
Dinah Shore saw a dinoshaur
bugger

Silver Jubilee Tribute

Twenty-five years older
Twenty-five years richer
With her diamond grin
And a wave of her fin –
There goes Lizzie

What Is Poetry?
(for Sasho, Daniella, Vladko and Martin Shurbanov)

Look at those naked words dancing together!
Everyone's very embarrassed.
Only one thing to do about it –
Off with your clothes
And join in the dance.
Naked words and people dancing together.
There's going to be trouble.
Here come the Poetry Police!

Keep dancing.

Autumnobile

The forest's throat is sore.
Frost-work. Echoing shouts of friends.
October, in her gold-embroidered nightie,
Floating downstream, little mad flowers shimmering.

The silky fur of her
And her hot fingers curling,
Uncurling round and a sudden shove –
There goes my heart tobogganing,

Down snow, slush, ending stuck in the mud,
That's love! O dig me out of here
And glide me off down Pleasure Street
To the sparkle rink where bears go skating.

I ate pancakes at the funeral.
I ate pancakes and ice-cream too.
The mourners drank like musty flies,
All round Summer's coffin, sucking and buzzing.

The days of dust and nights of gnats
Are over and, covered with raindrop warts,
My friend, the most unpopular Season in school,
Smoking and spitting – Autumn's coming.

How do I love that fool, the Fall?
Like Paraquatted nettles. Like
A two-headed 50p. Like a sick shark.
Like a punchy boxer who can't stop grinning.

Sunshine's rationed. Get in the queue
For a yard of colour, a pound of warm.
Deathbed scenes on the video-sky,
Sunsets like Olivier acting dying.

I feel weightless as a child who's built
Out of nursery bricks with ducks and clocks on.
I eat more sleep. I slap more feet.
Autumn – my marzipan flesh is seething.

I open a book and splash straight into it.
The fire reads all my old newspapers.
I freak across the galaxy on Pegasus
And see the cracked old world, rocking and bleeding.

The saloon doors in my skull swing open,
Out stride a posse of cowboy children
Bearing a cauldron of the magic beans
Which always set my poems quivering.

Now my electric typer purrs,
And now it clackers under my fingers'
Flickering. And now the oily engine
Throbs into hubbub. The Autumnobile is leaving.

Nobody on earth knows where on earth they're going
......

(a hell of a long way after Pushkin and Derzhavin)

Land of Dopes and Loonies

William Shakespeare was loony
Burns was a maniac too
Milton was thoroughly crackers
Yeats was a loony all through
Edward Lear, Shelley and Coleridge,
Whitman and Lawrence and Blake
What a procession of nutters
Looning for poetry's sake
All of the poets were dafties
Dafter when the going got rough
All except William Wordsworth
Who wasn't nearly crazy enough

Leonardo was loopy
So was Toulouse Lautrec
Bosch had all of his screws loose
Van Gogh's head was a wreck
Pablo Picasso was batty
Just take a look at his work
Rembrandt was out of his windmill
Brueghel was bloody berserk
All of the painters were bonkers
In the barmy army of art
All except Sir Joshua Reynolds
And he was a wealthy old Humpty Dumpty...

Land of DOPES and LOONIES

143

To a Critic

You don't go to Shakespeare for statistics
You don't go to bed for a religious service
But you want poems like metal mental mazes –
Excuse me while I nervous.

A song can carry so many facts
A song can lift plenty of story
A song can score jokes and curses too
And any amount of glory

But if you overload your dingadong song
With theoretical baggage
Its wings tear along the dotted line
And it droppeth to earth like a cabbage

Yes it droppeth to earth like a bloody great cabbage
And the cabbage begins to rot.
My songs may be childish as paper planes
But they glide – so thanks a lot.

A Sunset Cloud Procession Passing Ralph Steadman's House

1. A cigar-smoking porker drags a small hay-cart from which a jewelled crocodile smiles and waves.

2. A black fried egg struts by, one woolly eyebrow raised like Noel Coward.

3. An emaciated caribou clanks along.

4. An ant-eater inflates a smoker's-lung balloon.

5. Eskimo Jim pulls Auntie Hippo tail-first, but she hangs on to her perambulator full of hippolets.

6. They are pursued by a neolithic Hoover.

7. And followed by Leonardo's Tin Lizzie and Michelangelo as a tumescent frogman, pride of the Sexual Boat Service.

8. A simple mushroom shape, rising one inch every four seconds.

9. Father Time with a crumpled scythe.

10. A whale spouting black shampoo all over its own humpy head.

11. A cocker spaniel taking a free ride on the backbone of a boa-constrictor.

12. And up from out of the dark hill's shoulders rise the shoulders of another, larger, darker hill.

Smilers

When Woody Allen smiles
From the attics of the town
The secretary tears
Come rolling down

When John Wayne smiles
Boy you better grin
Or he'll be obliged
To kick your feelings in

About Suffering They Were Never Wrong the Old Mistresses

Bessie Smith
And Big Joe Turner
Make Othello
Sound like a learner

Ode to George Melly

If Bonzo the Dog got resurrected he could leap like you
If Satan the Snake ate Adam's birthday cake he would creep like you
If Liz Bat Queen wasn't pound-note green she'd hand the Crown to you –
For nothing on earth falls down like George Melly do.

Daydream Number 157,423

In a quiet afternoon drinking club
In a leather-upholstered booth
I wish I was listening to Billie Holiday
Telling the poisonous truth

First Poem Composed in a Dream

A snub-nosed woman holding a jug;
Maybe it will be empty
By 1969 or nineteen-sempty...

Second Poem Composed in a Dream

'Let's get married!'

'But I can't remember my name.'

'Let's get suffocated then!'

For the Eightieth Birthday of Hoagy Carmichael

(22 November 1979)

Hoagland – white waterfall piano keys!
Old rockin' chairs to help us all think mellow!
Always-Fall forests of star-tall trees
Growing chords of gold, brown, red and yellow!
Yes, Hoagland, friendliest of all countries.

Casual is, I guess, as casual does,
And you casually sing and casually knock us sideways.
Rolling songs riding the river's tideways,
Mist-songs gliding, city-songs that buzz.
I wander Hoagland pathways when dusk falls.
Celia strolls with me as wild and tame
Hoagland bird-folk enchant us with their calls.
Anyone who has ears grins at your name.
Eighty years of great songs! I wish you would
Live on as long as your good Hoagland life feels good.

NOTES:
a. Hoagland is Mr Carmichael's official Christian name
b. Celia is my wife's name.

To Elizabeth Quinn on the First Night
of *Children of a Lesser God* in London

(25 August 1981)

Tonight I saw a thousand birds
   Nobody knew their names
A thousand birds in flight
   a thousand birds
Tonight I saw a thousand birds

Happy Fiftieth Deathbed

D.H. Lawrence on the dodgem cars
Sniffing the smell of the electric stars
Cool black angel jumps up beside
Sorry David Herbert it's the end of your ride

Thank you very much Mr D.H. Lawrence
Thank you very much
Thank you very much Mr D.H. Lawrence
For *The Rainbow* and such

D.H. Lawrence with naughty Mrs Brown
Trying to play her hurdy-gurdy upside-down
In comes Mr Brown and he says Veronica
May I accompany on my harmonica

Thank you very much Mr D.H. Lawrence
Thank you very much
Thank you very much Mr D.H. Lawrence
Back to your hutch

D.H. Lawrence met Freud in a dream
Selling stop me and buy one Eldorado ice cream
Siggie says you ought to call your stories
Knickerbocker Splits and Banana Glories

Thank you very much Mr D.H. Lawrence
Thank you very much
Thank you very much Mr D.H. Lawrence
Keep in touch

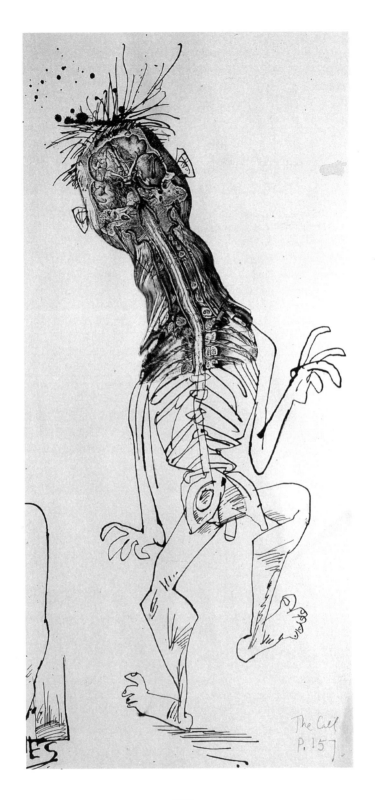

The Call
P. 157

The Call
(*or* Does The Apple Tree Hate Plums?)

i was standing in my room
the whirling tape was singing:
i'm never going back
i'm never going back.

i read four lines by Elaine Feinstein
the tears jumped in my eyes.
i read eight lines by Allen Ginsberg
and electricity sprang
from the soles of my feet
and the electric flames
danced on the roof of my skull.

someone calling
my self calling to myself
the call i'd been hoping for

let yourself sing it said
let yourself dance
let yourself be
an apple tree

i wrote this daftness down
then smiled and smiled
and said aloud
thank you thank you

you may want money
you may want pears
you may want bayonets
or tears

shake me as hard as you like
only apples will fall
apples   apples   and apples

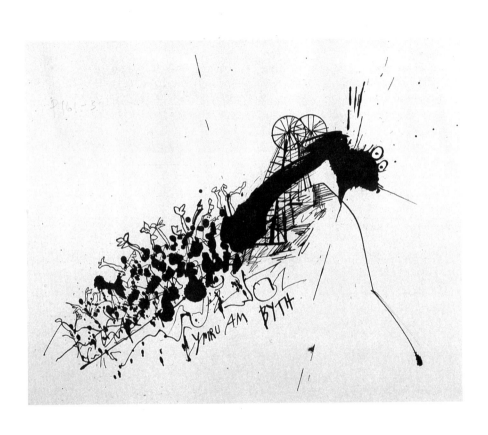

CYMRU AM BYTH

Lament for the Welsh Makers

WILLIAM DUNBAR sang piteously
When he mourned for the Makers of poetry.
He engraved their names with this commentary –
Timor mortis conturbat me.

DUNBAR, I'm Scot-begotten too,
But I would celebrate a few
Welsh masters of the wizardry –
The fear of death moves inside me.

'After the feasting, silence fell.'
ANEIRIN knew how the dead smell.
Now he has joined their company.
The fear of death moves inside me.

TALIESIN, born of earth and clay,
Primroses, the ninth wave's spray
And nettle flowers, where is he?
The fear of death moves inside me.

LLYWARCH's sons numbered twenty-four.
Each one was eaten by the war.
He lived to curse senility.
The fear of death moves inside me.

TALHAEARN and AROFAN,
AFAN FERDDIG and MORFRAN
Are lost, with all their poetry.
The fear of death moves inside me.

MYRDDIN sang, a silver bell,
But from the battlefield he fell
Into a deep insanity.
The fear of death moves inside me.

GWALCHMAI, who sang of Anglesey
And a girl like snowfall on a tree
And lions too, lies silently –
The fear of death moves inside me.

CYNDDELW's balladry was sold
For women's kisses and men's gold.
His shop is shut permanently.
The fear of death moves inside me.

HYWEL chanted Meirionnydd's charm.
His pillow was a girl's white arm.
Now he is whiter far than she.
The fear of death moves inside me.

PRYDYDD Y MOCH would smile to see
An Englishman – if he was maggoty.
Now he is grinning bonily.
The fear of death moves inside me.

DAFYDD AP GWILYM did women much good
At the cuckoo's church in the green wood.
Death ended his sweet ministry.
The fear of death moves inside me.

GWERFYL MECHAIN wrote in cheerful tones
Of the human body's tropical zones.
She shared DAFYDD's hot philosophy.
The fear of death moves inside me.

IOLO GOCH wrote of any old thing –
Girls, feasts and even an English King.
They say he died most professionally.
The fear of death moves inside me.

GRUFFUDD GRYG wept desperately
For the North of Wales in her poverty.
He was a bird from heaven's country.
The fear of death moves inside me.

LLYWELYN GOGH's fist dared to knock
On the heavy door with the black steel lock.
A skull told him its history.
The fear of death moves inside me.

SION CENT, who sang thank you to his purse,
RHYS GOGH, who killed a fox with verse,
Sleep in the gravel dormitory.
The fear of death moves inside me.

IEUAN AP RHYDDERCH so scholarly,
GWERFUL MADOG of famed hospitality,
LEWYS GLYN COTHI who loved luxury –
The fear of death moves inside me.

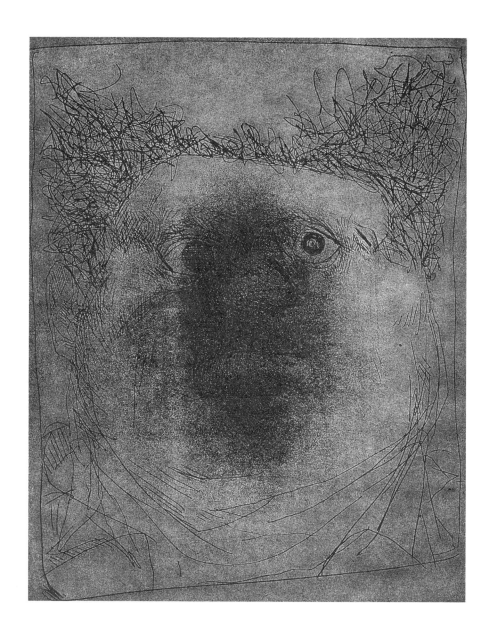

DAFYDD AP EDMWND's singing skill
Thrilled through all Wales. Then it fell still.
LEWYS MON wrote his elegy.
The fear of death moves inside me.

BEDO BRWNLLYS, IEUAN DEULWYN,
GUTYN OWAIN, TUDUR PENLLYN,
All exiles in Death's monarchy.
The fear of death moves inside me.

Life was dark-coloured to TUDUR ALED.
WILLIAM LLYN brooded on the dead.
SION TUDUR mocked all vanity.
The fear of death moves inside me.

DIC HUWS dedicated a roundelay
To a girl by the name of Break of Day.
Night broke on both of them, remorselessly –
The fear of death moves inside me.

And hundreds have since joined the towering choir –
Poets of Wales, like trees on fire,
Light the black twentieth century.
The fear of death moves inside me.

Oh DYLAN THOMAS, as bright as nails,
Could make no kind of a living in Wales
So he died of American charity.
The fear of death moves inside me.

Terror of death, terror of death,
Terror of death, terror of death,
That drumbeat sounds relentlessly.
The fear of death moves inside me.

Since we must all of us ride down
The black hill into the black town,
Let us sing out courageously.
The fear of death moves inside me.

The black lungs swell, the black harp sighs,
Whenever a Welsh maker dies.
Forgive my nervous balladry.
Timor mortis conturbat me.

LOVe, The APEMAN, CURSES, Blessings and FRIENDS

Good Day

the day was like molten glass
i sauntered around with a carnival heart
picking up the puppies other people threw away
and arranging them in my pouch

yes the day was like molten glass
so i took my spade down the old peninsula
dug a channel across its neck and watched the sea jump through
then drank to the health of a new island

well the day was like molten glass
sunshine greeting me like a big irish doctor
blackberries tapping out a rhythm on their leaves
tight enough and bright enough to set a donkey dancing

i said the day was like molten glass
the fingers of the cruising breezes
massaged the tensions out of my head
and i loved my love with an a and an ab and everything down to zed

Celia Celia

When I am sad and weary
When I think all hope has gone
When I walk along High Holborn
I think of you with nothing on

Footnotes on Celia Celia

Used to slouch along High Holborn
in my gruesome solo lunch-hours.
It was entirely lined
with Gothick insurance offices
except for one oblong block of a shop
called Gamages,
where, once,
drunk, on Christmas Eve,
I bought myself a battery-operated Japanese pig
with a chef's hat on top of his head
and a metal stove which lit up red
and the pig moved a frying pan up and down with his hand
and tossed a plastic fried egg into the air
and caught it again the other way up
and then tossed it and caught it again and again
all the time emitting squeals of excitement
through a series of holes in the top of his head –

but apart from that…I want to forget High Holborn.

September Love Poem

I flop into our bed with Thee,
Ovaltine and warm milk-o
And there we lie in ecstasy
Watching Sergeant Bilko.

The Accountant in His Bath

The accountant dried his imperfect back
As he stood in the sinking water –
'In ten years' time I'll be dead as cork,
No sooner, no later.

'Numbers display more muscle every day,
They multiply while I'm asleep.
When I fall to pieces they won't even see,
They'll keep on adding each other up.

'I know the numbers, each has a colour,
Twenty-three is olive green,
Five's a comedian (all have characters),
One is God and eight's the Queen.

'But I was never envious of numbers,
Watching them replace each other;
Like the grim wolves, not one remembers
His fading father.

'Passionless, lean, their armies march,
Invade more ledgers, take more men alive;
But they're not free to run or lurch
Each to his private grave.'

Patches of water shrank inside the bath.
Confident in the immortal numbers
He heard his wife's amazing laugh;
'I love her,' he said, as he pulled on his pyjamas.

All Fool's Day

A man sits counting the days of Spring.
His hands may tremble but his mind won't stir,
And one thought runs through all his watching:
'I would have burnt my heart for her.

'If she had recognised my face
As I knew hers, and listened to me sing,
I would have left the careless human race
For one hour of her careful loving.

'When spring swings round again, and I am here,
I will forget the terrors of her voice –
But I would stay with terror at my ear
And burn my heart, if I had any choice.'

Riddle

Their tongues are knives, their forks are hands and feet.
They feed each other through their skins and eat
Religiously the spiced, symbolic meat.
The loving oven cooks them in its heat –
Two curried lovers on a rice-white sheet.

Take Stalk Between Teeth Pull Stalk From Blossom Throw Blossom Overarm Towards Enemy Lie Flat And Await Explosion

I staggered in the garage and handed them my heart.
'Can you overhaul it cos the bloody thing won't start?'
They hammered it and sprayed it till it looked just like a toad,
They told me that it shouldn't be allowed on the road.
They said I'd better trade it for a psych-e-del-ic screen.
They said 'What d'you call this aboriginal machine?'
I said
It's a rose I suppose.

A unicorn is bathing in the shallows of your eyes.
You've got a mouth that's whispering between your thighs
You bring me foreign honeycombs and science fiction ties
And every time you touch me you declare your surprise.
Your language is a code that I haven't yet cracked
So I can't be sure of your message or a fact
But
It's a rose I suppose.

When they see us walking, they're puzzled what to say.
We're so obvious in a mysterious way –
Clouds that fly south when the wind goes east,
Hovercraft feet and faces all creased
We draw our wages in musical wine
And what our business is, well that's harder to define
But
It's a rose I suppose.

Well Tennyson's on television selling bad breath.
Lyndon's in the pulpit and the sermon is death.
Hitler's in the bunker playing nuclear chess,
Judas got a column on the *Sunday Express*.
The zombies are lurching all over the town,
There's only one weapon seems to bring them all down
And
It's a rose I suppose.

162

A Wise Woman

Woman called Sarah born with nothing but looks and lust
I saw her on her deathbed she was smiling fit to bust
She said: I've lived my life on the Golden Triangle plan –
Don't play with razors, don't pay your bills, don't boogie with a married man.

For Julietta, Who Asked for an Epitaph

The half-dead shone with double life
When magicked by her liveliness.
Over the woods she used to go
Flying in her flying dress.

But Death was depressed.
He took Julietta.
She smiled and danced with him.
Now Death feels better.

Top-Notch Erotic Moment Thank You

the slime was soaking through my khaki
barbed wire scratching the star-bomb sky
my rifle was heavy as Europe
as i prayed to the snipers for a Blighty
then her breast brushed my shoulder

a thousand thousand lights were clicking at each other
yes the galaxies inside my head were coming good
and i was a visionary scientist on the verge
of creating a multi-versal language and a source of free food
then her breast brushed my shoulder

i was studying despair in Kentish Town Road
and i began to envy a torn cardboard box saying Oxo
being blown along the gutter by a tough November
in the general direction of Euston Station
then her breast brushed my shoulder

now i sit in a dark armchair and think about it
and first i smile about it and then i nearly cry about it
and i know i'm so knotted i'll do nothing about it
but write these lines to remind me of how my ribs went twang
when her breast brushed my shoulder

Coming Back

this auburn autumn
this free-for-all
free-fall fall

the trees are making so much money
that the river's bulging with gold

and i'm coming back to life,
                              love,
i'm coming back to leaf

The Angels in Our Heads

Our angels, spiralling,
Climb the sky like two, like one,
With wings flowing and easy-going
Rippling the current of the sun.

Altitude one hundred miles.
Our angels level out and hover,
Humming delirious pop songs,
Quivering at each other.

Silent suddenly, they shrug
Their rainbow wings around each other.
A thousand multi-coloured hairs
Vibrate along each feather.

And then they drop.
Birds in crowds
Watch and admire from
Grandstand clouds.

The angels both spreadeagle, braking,
Over the ocean, gold and deep.
They slide into its heated waters
To sing in bubbles in their sleep.

Waking, they wander underwater,
Gulping the seasoned sea food, free,
Then they take off in fifty yards
Sprinting across the surface of the sea,

Circling waterbirds, circling higher,
Those weighty feathers dry, and then
Zoom up to a hundred miles
And – there they go again.

But when they look out through our eyes
To see the rain piercing like wire
Or the white wind throw hurtful snow
Burying men in drifts of pain and fire

Sometimes our angels hunch and huddle,
Grounded, sad ducks stuck.
But they should moult and stomp outside,
Socialists fighting dirty luck.

For they can talk or march against the winter,
Get home in time for aerobatics, try
To teach their children to be flyers and swimmers
In a warm planet with a cleaner sky.

All Night Long

SUNDREAM
     SUNSLEEP
NIGHTBREAK   you
     MOONFLOW   are
STARFLIGHT   asleep
     MOONSET   beside
LIGHTGATHER   me
     DAYFALL

Out

when I broke the light bulb an orange dropped out
when I peeled the orange a rabbit jumped out
when I shook the rabbit a parcel dropped out
when I opened the parcel your house fell out
when I rang the doorbell you were out

A Girl Called Music

A girl called Music
She drifts where she's not allowed.
She can do a soft-shoe-shuffle
On an illuminated cloud.
She's the imaginary milkmaid
To the snorers in city attics.
Her eye is the porthole of the washing machine
In which a coat of many colours does acrobatics –

    She makes the bread rise
    And the Sun go sideways
    My tender submarine
    Adores her tideways –

To a Godly Man

Don't waffle to me about Kingdom Come
I've often loitered there.
My left hand was on Celia's bum,
My right hand in her hair.

Hello Adrian
(for Adrian Henri)

Hello Adrian – I just crawled out the far side of Xmas to scrawl my report
                  on the wall
We breathed nothing but wine all the time till the group got liquidated on the
                  twelfth day with turkey soup.
Well it was a feast of the beast and half the animals were kissing
                  when they weren't pissing
Though there were days when the haze turned jagged and I walked into a room
                  full of stainless smiles and white tiles –

                  But I will confess
I never had it
                  Halfway up a pylon
Never had it
                  Under the stage during a performance of Ibsen's
                  An Enemy of the People
Never had it
                  In the Whispering Gallery at St Paul's
Never had it
                  Up against a parking meter

                  But where – it doesn't matter
                  When – it doesn't count
                  All you got to total
                  Is the total amount

                  They're doing it for peace
                  Doing it for war
                  There's only one good reason
                  For doing it for

                  CHORUS:
                  Fuck for fun (Fuck fuck fuck for fun)
                  Fuck for fun (Fuck fuck fuck for fun)
                  Fuck for fun (Fuck fuck fuck for fun)
                  Everybody want to (boom boom)
                  Fuck for fun.

                  They're doing it in Paris
                  'Cos it taste so sweet
                  They do it by the Mersey
                  'Cos they like that beat

They doing it for Mother
Doing it for Freud
Reginald Plantagenet
Somerset-Boyd

(CHORUS)

They do it for publicity
Doing it for cash
Might as well be robots
The way they bash

They do it in Chicago
Just to fool the fuzz
They do it down in London
Just 'cos Mick Jagger does

(CHORUS)

They do it up in Edinburgh
With cannon balls
Newcastle girls do it
High on the walls

Now there's too little action
Too much talk
When the bottle's open
Throw away the cork

(CHORUS)

Well North Riding girls taste of cedarwood
South Riding girls cook the wildest pud
East Riding girls melt your soul like lard
West Riding girls well they try bloody hard
North East West South side by side
What you care so long as they ride
So ride your lover
Get on your little lover and ride

They do it in the Palace
To preserve the line
But we're going to do it
'Cos it feels so fine

I've got a red-hearted woman
I'm a socialist man
We've got a great leap forward
And a five year plan

(CHORUS)

An eye for an eye
Tit for tat
Batman fuck Robin
And Robin fuck a bat

Fuck for fun (Fuck fuck fuck for fun)
Fuck for fun (Fuck fuck fuck for fun)
Doesn't matter if you're incredibly old or absurdly young
C'mon everybody and (boom boom)
Fuck for fun.

The Collected WORKS

of APEMAN MUDGEON

Apeman Keep Thinking It's Wednesday

Woken up in fork of tree
By usual jungle jangle
No tom-toms.
No metal bird
Full of Nazi paratroops.
Jumped down
THELONK!
Into turtle pool,
Splashed massive torso.
Searched for berries with mate.
Ate berries with mate and young.
Groomed mate. Groomed by mate.
Groomed young.
Sent young to learn
Ways of jungle.
Bashed chest with fists,
Gave mighty howl,
Loped off into undergrowth to hunt.
Lay along thick branch,
Saw longhorned poem approaching.
Dropped on poem's back,
Grabbed its neck.
Big poem, threw me off.
Bump on head.
Tried liana swinging.
Good swinging.
Ninth liana bad liana,
Dropped me on rock.
Ankle go blue.
At water-hole discussed crocodiles
With seminar of chimpanzees.
Inspected poem-traps.
Only found one squeaky poem
Without a tail.
Too small, let it go.
Limped back to tree.
Told mate and young
About head and ankle.
Mate said she caught fish.
Ate fish with mate and young.
Fish taste like a good poem.
Sent young up trunk into tree.
Mated with mate.

Climbed up trunk.
Lay down in fork of tree.
Huge moon.
Dreamed about a poem stampede.

The Apeman Who Hated Snakes

Was an apeman lived next door to me
In some kind of prickly tree.

That apeman had the angry shakes
Spending all his sleep in dreams about snakes.

And every morning he would shout
How all the snakes have to be stamp out.

Pastime he enjoy the best
Was to poke a stick down a mamba's nest

Or he'd have a slaughter down the old snake-pit
And look pretty happy at the end of it.

He tattooed snakes all over his skin
Coiling and hissing from knees to chin.

For breakfast he hard-boiled the eggs of snakes.
Suppertime – Boa-constrictor steaks.

For a man who hated reptiles so obsessively
He spend an awful lot of time in their company.

Now where that apeman lived next door to me
There's a vacancy in that prickly tree.

I reckon snakes are like me and you –
They got a mystery job to do.

So when I see one in my path I salute
And take a roundabout alternative route.

The Apeman's Hairy Body Song

Happy to be hairy
Happy to be hairy
When the breezes tickle
The hairs of my body

Happy to be hairy
Happy to be hairy
Next best thing
To having feathers

Apeman Gives a Poetry Reading

Apeman travel much in jungle
Sometimes he swing for many miles
To taxi down in some new clearing
No concert posters up on trees
Tiger who arranged the gig
Has gone down with sabre-tooth-ache.
Gazelle apologises nervously.
Apeman and gazelle shift rocks around
To form a semi-circle.
Two or three crocodiles trundle in.
Four flying squirrels. One sloth.
Various reptiles and a fruit-bat.
Suddenly – ten-eleven multi-colour birds.
Apeman cheers up.
Gazelle checks time by the sun,
Introduces apeman.
Apeman performs a series
Of variegated apeman howls –
Comic howls, sad howls, angry-desperate howls.
Apeman runs out of howl, sits down.
Senior crocodile asks questions:
What use is howling?
Howling does not change jungle.
Apeman stares at him,
Nods, shakes his head, gives up.
Animals begin to drift to holes and nests.

Apeman swings home heavily through the gloom.
If you meet apeman in this mood
Give him a hug.
Unless your name is Boa-constrictor.

It Ain't What They Do It's What the Apeman Do

What the gagmen do
the swagmen do
and the bagmen and the ragmen and the stagmen do

What the cashmen do
the bashmen do
and the flashmen and the crashmen and moustachemen do

do do do
altogether all the do do day
do do do
doing it the same old do do way

What the awful lawful
riflemen do
the shufflemen and trufflemen are doing it too

What the boo-hoo shoemen
and the bluemen do
the few human crewmen and bitumen men do

do do do
altogether all the do do day
do do do
doing it the same old do do way

But what the Apeman do
is what the Apeman do
except when he decides to do
something different from himself

175

The Apeman Recollects Emotion in Tranquillity with a Copy of the *TLS* Stuck Up His Arse

Jump that jungle
Jump that jungle
Pump that jungle
Pump that jungle
Eat that jungle
Eat that jungle
Heat that jungle
Heat that jungle
Joke that jungle
Joke that jungle
Soak that jungle
Soak that jungle
Sling that jungle
Sling that jungle
Sing that jungle
Sing that jungle
Grow that jungle
Grow that jungle

Blow that jungle
Blow that jungle
Make that jungle
Make that jungle
Shake that jungle
Shake that jungle
Climb that jungle
Climb that jungle
Chime that jungle
Chime that jungle
Plumb that jungle
Plumb that jungle
Come that jungle
Come that jungle
Shove that jungle
Shove that jungle
Love that jungle
Love that jungle
The jungle loves you

Apeman as Tourist Guide

Apeman show you round Jungle?
All right.

Big cliff with holes in
Is baboon high-rise development.
Dusty clearing
With banyan tree full of honking birds
Is discotheque for elephants.
Quick! Jump in water – breathe through hollow reed –
Safari party of lions going by.

Tell you something:
Apeman love this
Hot and rowdy jungle.
Tell you something else:
Jungle not all like this.

You keep on walking
And sooner or later
You will find the other jungle –

The frozen jungle.
Black ice
On every branch, tendril,
Pool, path, animal and man.

Black ice jungle
Where it's too cold
To see or hear
Too cold
To feel too cold to think
As heart and brains
Turn into black turn into ice.

Don't you worry.
Most of the jungle
Given over to
Sweaty celebration.
You may not stumble into
Black ice jungle
For years and years.

You like to see
River of boiling rock
Or giraffe motorway?
No? Got to catch boat?
Go well. Got any shiny discs
So Apeman can buy firewater?

Apeman's Science Fiction Dream

Apeman and Apewomen roll past galaxies
In warm, soft globe-ship.
Hairy body, smooth body,
In half-asleep, half-waking,
Non-stop, sliding, weightless love-play.

Their bubble craft
Shudders with happiness,
Slows right down
And sidles towards
An orange, heated planet
Shaped, on one side, like a belly,
Other side like a bum.
It revolves sensuously –
Belly, bum. Belly, bum.
Globe-ship and planet of Belly-Bum,
Smiling, smiling,
Draw together slowishly.

Gradually the Apeman's cock
Pushes its way out through the bubbleskin
And sinks, deep as it can, into the planet.
And from the surface of Belly-Bum,
An orange pop-up cock
Slides into Apewoman's wonder quim.

There will be two children from this union.
They will return to earth and save the earth.

The Apeman's Motives

He not hunt the poem for money –
The kind he catch fetch nowt.
He no hunt the poem for fun –
He not a very good sport.
Apeman go after poem
With fists and teeth and feet
Because he need the juices
Contained in the poem meat.

*   *   *

Confession

Of course I've been corrupted by publicity
A friendly journalist once likened me to Bogart
And I took to exposing my upper teeth when I smiled at enemies

Several years later I was in a theatre
At the same time as Lauren Bacall
And she was so beautiful I could only look at her for two seconds

And that was enough,
Sam, that was plenty.

Self-Congratulating, Self-Deprecating,
Auto-Destructive Blues

If you're betting on the horses, you know you've got to follow form
Got to vet up on the set-up and get up and bet on form,
I was losing losing losing before I was even born.

You may come from Venezuela, but I was born on Mars,
Venice or Venus or Venezuela, but I was raised on Mars,
I've got a head full of meteorites, heart full of little green children
and balls full of shooting stars.

So if you want a good investment, better not buy me.
I'm on the edge of the ledge and I'm not gilt-edge so your broker will
advise I'm a joker so get wise and don't buy me.
Some men are like insurance, but I'm more like – suck it and see.

I Passed for Sane

If I'd been born without a mind
I would be happy, tame and kind.
People came, saying good things.
So many people, saying good things.
I hid my eyes under my skin
And so they never saw right in.

Sometimes I Feel Like a Childless Mother

My hands shake, my eyelids tremble.
The tigers in my head assemble.

The Open Savage

the open savage
enters a roomful of coded conversation
the open savage
hides underneath himself

the open savage
is invaded by visions
the open savage
sings embarrassingly

the open savage
attends a logical dissection of the universe
the open savage
weeps as he throws baked beans at the platform

the open savage
does not explain himself
the open savage
is himself

the open savage
is accused of being open
the open savage
smiles like a jar of honey with no lid

The Institution

The crazy talkers in my head
Steal lights and moments when they can;
Beat at the windows to be fed
Or listen to the sounds of rain.
They stroll, they shout at passing Man,
And in extremes they form a plan
To drown at night, or catch a train.

Simple as glass, they wander through
The colours of my twenty years
Singing and whispering the true
And false of all my private cares;
Inflated songs that shrink to fears.
My chest is thick, so no one hears
The lovely mute who kicks and tears...

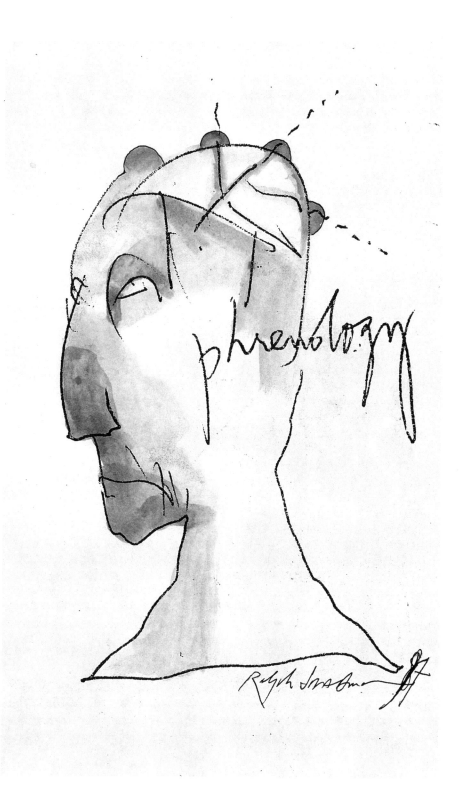

phrenology

Daydream One

Nobel Maths Wizards Make Odd Discovery –
Two and Two Makes Five And a Bit.
Schoolkids Burn Dummies of Einstein and Newton
As they chant:
Two and Two Makes Five And a Bit.
Bridges collapse   Skyscrapers sway and fold
Cash registers and computers in mass suicide
Thames full of stockbrokers and taxmen

Only the average people
whose maths is so far below average
go about their normal unbusinesslike business
making things without measuring them exactly,
buying Two and Two
and being charged Five And a Bit.

Daydream Two

At nine or was it nineteen,
I was the Invisible Man.
Great thing about being the Invisible Man
Is you can watch girls undressing.
At nine or was it nineteen
I was crazy to watch girls undressing.

What I did was this –
Wait for a warm day, because
The Invisible Man can't wear any clothes.
Then, hang about the street in Esher, say,
Till a nice-looking girl walked by.
Then I'd start to follow her home.
Sometimes she'd climb into a car
And drive away over the horizon.
When my luck was in she'd walk straight home
And I'd manage, by posing as a strong wind,
To slip into her house as she opened the door.

Then I'd hang around in corners before she decided,
About four in the morning, to go to bed.
If I was out of luck, she'd undress in the dark.
With luck I'd see her take off her clothes.
Wow!

Trouble is, this made me randy,
Well that was, in a way, the point,
But I felt pretty tentative
About making an invisible proposition.
So I'd start: Look please don't be frightened but –

EEEK EEEEK!

And suddenly her little bedroom would be filled
By her father, Goliath, carrying a poker,
Swinging it round his head and shouting:
I've cornered that bloody daydreamer –
I'll give him Invisible bloody Man!

A Slow Boat to Trafalgar

I was born in a country called Bloody Strange
With the means of seduction, prostitution and derange
I was red all through and I was raw on top
I had a billion megatons and nowhere to drop
I was a suitable case
A suitable case
A suitable case for
Urgghh.

Married ten times to the gulp next door
She was twenty to virgin and half past whore
We had a mini monster and we called him Meat
And he sucked our cold sweat through a teat
He was a suitable case
A suitable case
A suitable case for
Aaragghh.

Martian mother and Venusian father
But I tadpoled out of the shaving lather
Here come the State chewing Gandhi on toast
Send your subscriptions to the Roly-Poly Ghost
He's an accusable suit
An unstable goose
A two-sable sake for
Raarhh.

A Machine That Makes Love and Poems and Mistakes

The whirring stops, the door in my chest
Slides open. Fatty squeezes out
Smiling like silver. An airliner staircase
Appears under his first step. He podges down
Applauding himself with padded palms.

Next Jagged, wearing his frayed-wire suit,
Scales my legs, jerks through the door and pulls
My starting handle. Thought-gears grind.
He's muddled, pressing all my buttons
Too hard. Not hard enough. His blood is caffeine.

He exits limping, gladly. Then he flops
Prone on the tarmac, hiding his splintered eyes.
His place is taken. This one's a prodigy,
A milk-faced boy of five who sings to himself
As he tries to play tunes with knobs and levers.

I've got other mechanics. Sometimes they fight
Over my delicate controls. They strike,
Or try to make me fly. They blow my fuses.
Just now I didn't answer. You caught me between shifts.
Ask again now. Someone will answer you.

Snow Wheat, Snow What?

dopey sneezy grumpy
happy doc er bashful

but i couldn't remember
the name of dwarf seven

there must be some freudy reason
my consciousness is trying to hide
from my dirty old subconscious

dopey sneezy grumpy
happy doc um bashful

who made a getaway?
was it –

      greasy?
      majesty?
      mummy?
      anarchy?

all of the reference books were dumb
even the bible and debrett

the name came by combusteous spontaneon –

      sleepy

it was three twenty-six in the afternoon
so i went to bed and dozed like seven dwarfs
after all that
think think think think think think think
hi ho hi ho it's off to sleep i go

187

Holding My Water Under Breath

Washed my skin and shaved my chin and washed my skin again.
   My suit was suavely dark and darkly suave.
   I joined a constellation
Of the washed white, the suavely shaven.

martini, martini, martini, martini, martini, martini.

   My skull was a martini glass,
   My brain the olive.
My face began to dirt over, to sprout stubble.
   I werewolfed.
Happily, I began to make trouble.

Toy Stone

I dived and found it.

A wedge of stone,
Grey mixed with the mauve
Of sky before snow.
Flakes of crystal
Shining among its mineral clouds.

Now and again I look at the stone,
Convert it into the relief map
Of a nude island or the night sky.
Or use it as a racquet
For bouncing light into my eyes.

Today I took it with my eyes shut.
Turning the stone between my hands
I learned
That it shares the shape and weight
Of a small pistol.

Now it has a barrel,
A chamber and a butt.
Held by the barrel, it could be used
To bash almost anything to death.
Stone-shine is in my head,
But so is the killing weight of the stone.

Toy stone, weapon stone.
I will keep it.

Unfulfilled Suicide Note

because there is a golden plastic arrow on the desk in front of me
because my stomach is heavy and drags downwards
because I cannot find anything
because I cannot understand anything
because I am afraid of everyone
because there is a small amount of snow on the ground outside

We Moved to a Farmhouse in the Yorkshire Dales and Look What Happened

Let your soul roll around these horizons,
An unchipped marble with clouds inside
Buzzing around the huge green bowl of meadows.

We sleepwalk, musically, down the tunnels of this grey rock
Which was excavated by a painstaking Jacobean drunk
Who hewed out slit-eyed bedrooms and the largest bathroom in the world.

It all looks as easy as the pink felt pig
Which lies so sideways between the upended Czech projection screen
And the solid leather suitcase which holds no more than a monochrome postcard.

It all looks gigantic as our first washing machine
Which shakes the landscape, whose brand-name is Jehovah.
This morning, out of its dirty-water gut, the machine produced

A synthesis of Marx Freud Blake Dylan Us in two hundred words,
A small creature, like a golden dog but the size of an ant
And a shower of what I thought at first were hundreds and thousands
But which hurtled towards the outstretched window
In the direction of the ionosphere. I caught one of them,
Held it for a fifteenth of a second before it burned its way through
The palm of my hand, between the finger bones, and up up and away.

It was, I noted, a miniature planet
Called Grain or Groin or Groan or something like that

And I saw, in that fleck of a moment, before it joined the flock
Of other confectionary planets, all the creatures on its surface
And they were, you know, they were like we want to be.

And then the speck-sized planet flared away from me
    And it rolled, like a soul, around these horizons,
    An unchipped marble with clouds inside,
    Buzzing around this huge green bowl of meadows.

And Some Lemonade Too

Drinking gin eating curry
That's my second favourite game
Begin feeling hollow
Then you sip and swallow
Till they start to taste about the same
Well gin got a bite
Curry got a burn
Try to teach your tongue to take them in turn
Drinking gin eating curry
Shoobi doobi wah wah

Drinking gin eating curry
Feeling my way to my ease
When the curry was dead
The gin hit my head
Till I fell down on my knees
Curry's ambrosia
Gin is the elixir
I am the champion concrete-mixer
Eating gin drinking curry
Shoobi doobi wah wah

Drinking gin eating curry
Gulped down all my trouble
Spent a magical sleep
In a happy old heap
And woke up with chutney-flavour alcohol stubble
Took a look at heaven
Took a look at hell
Reckoned I fancied them equally well
Sinking gin and beating curry
Wah wah shoobi doobi wah wah wah

It's Five O'Clock in the Morning

a blob-eyed platypus wallows and waddles
down in the hollow an adder's egg addles
as an albatross shits the colour of christmas
all over our bountiful bicycle saddles

It's a Clean Machine

(to the Beatles and Albert Hunt)

A cop needs a gangster, gangsters need cops,
Fire against fire and it never stops,
But I don't want a fire, I've got underskin heating
Thank you.

They know what we're afraid of:
Soundproof cellars, rhinoceros hide,
Genital electrodes, kneecap sledgehammers,
The moment when they take off your shoes –
All of the commonplace terrors.
But I won't name my own special fears,
Thank you.

I have been a one-man band to the galaxies over Bradford
As I skated over the rust-coloured pavements singing:

  Ten cents a dance, that's what they pay me
  A four-legged friend, a four-legged friend, he'll never let you down.
  Oh you can knock me down, stamp on my face, slander my name
  all over the place
  But we'll meet again, don't know where, don't know when –
  There is a laughing policeman, lives along our street,
  You can hear him laughing, when he's on the beat –
  Oh R, I say R-A,
  R-A-T, R-A-T-T,
  R-A-T-T-F, R-A-T-T-F-I-N-K,
  Ratfink (brawawa) Ratfink (brawawa),
  Mona Lisa Mona Lisa men have named you
  So squeeze my lemon baby till the juice runs down my leg –

Singing dangerously
As I bulged with the dynamite sticks of love.
They never caught me yet, but they keep trying.

It happens every day.
I'm standing down the lavatory end
Of a shadow-inhabited bar
When in walks the winter gangster-cop
And everyone he passes is gripped by his metal hand
And they wince as the grip tightens
And their faces sag as the grip relaxes.

The loudspeaker says:
An invitation to the glittering world of Robert Farnon –
Then he acts.
His icicles focus on my eyes.
Capone or Fabian, he yawns.
His iced knees, like car bumpers,
persuade me to the glittering pavement
Where his wide-shouldered Mercedes waits to eat me.
So far, so bad.

But they never warned him at headquarters,
They never told him the end of the story,
They never told him the way it always ends.

For here they come, sudden surrounders,
All of them laughing, all around us,
The gentle, fire-fighting cavalry,
House-high on ladders, crouched to hydrants,
Flashing their scarlet down the boulevard,
Hoses jumping with the pressure of water from
A thousand Welsh waterfalls, a hundred thousand lochs,
Aiming their polished, jerking nozzles –

And here I wish I could record all of their names but they know who they
are, the men and women and children I love and those who love me and may
the two lists always coincide –

All my friends, crimson, helmeted, hatchet-holstered.
Their hoses slosh him down slush-flushing gutters and:
I'm sorry Adrian, I'm sorry, he drizzles,
I didn't know you were a member of the Fire Brigade.

The Sun Likes Me

'The sun likes me' – Spanish way of saying 'I like the sun'

The sun likes me.
Maybe I've been lying out in the Mayakovsky too long.
Maybe my mind's been a breast-stroke commuter between London and
New York too long.
Maybe I've been longing too long.

The sun likes me.
Maybe it's because my dynamic tension comic-strip bible hath taught me that
it's better to kick sand into the sunlight and watch how it shimmers
than kick it in a twenty-stone muscleman's face.
And maybe it's because my atoms won't stand still because they want to rock
and roll all over the place –

But she taught me to say it.
I was near enough to lick her
And I licked her like the sun licks me and
WOW
She was a buxom anchovy.
Through both our sunrise sunset bodies I heard her say:
'Repeat it after me –
The sun likes me.'
So I said it (and I believe it):
The sun likes me.
I woke up full of business.
After a two-day year at the Registry of Companies I discovered that a 61 per
cent majority on the board of the sun was held by a holding company
(Sol Investments) represented by Phoebus Nominees who were
nominated by a legalistic fabrication called Icarus Consolidation
half-immersed in liquidation.
And the only stockholder –
Thanks to Auntie Irma's will –
The only stockholder
Was ME.
I seem to have changed.
The sun likes me.
I'm indifferent.
The sun doesn't like me.
See if I care.
For like it or lump it,
I own it.

Last week I found I'd left my Barclaycard in *Das Kapital* but when the bill
came round I simply reached into my asbestos wallet, produced the aforesaid
golden disc or orb and you should have seen the faces of the waiters or their
feet for that matter as they blushed to the colour of burnt semolina –

> Because I own the sun,
> The only one.
> Mine, mine,
> Sixty-one per cent of it,
>   MINE.

Self Critic

who is it trips me in the jig?
she wears a cast-iron dress
and growls because i can't recall her name –
my heavy-heartedness.

it's Radio 2, it's after-flu,
it's the Water Board's statement to the Press,
it's the sonic boom above the toothache room –
my heavy-heartedness.

got a weighty parcel shaped like awkwardness
wrapped in slippery plastic stuff.
trying to get my hands to clasp around it
but my arms aren't quite lengthy enough.
everybody thinks i'm carrying a bomb
but it's a book from a beautiful press.
oh the rain gets chiller and the buses get fuller
and the forecast – heavy-heartedness.

who's that extra-awful character in my plays
from the SS Officer's Mess
who makes hour-long speeches that you can't quite hear?
my heavy-heartedness.

so if I sink in the drink and sing *Sentimental Journey*
and then clown and fall down in a mess,
i'm just trying to kick that gangster out of my soul –
my heavy-heartedness.

Adrian Mitchell's Famous Weak Bladder Blues

Now some praise God because he gave us the bomb to drop in 1945
But I thank the Lord for equipping me with the fastest cock alive.

You may think a sten-gun's frequent, you can call greased lightning fast,
But race them down to the Piccadilly bog and watch me zooming past.

> Well it's excuse me,
> And I'll be back.
> Door locked so ra-a-tat-tat.
> You mind if I go first?
> I'm holding this cloudburst.
> I'll be out in 3.7 seconds flat.

I've got the Adamant Trophy, the Niagara Cup, you should see me on the M1 run,
For at every comfort station I've got a reputation for – doing the ton.

Once I met that Speedy Gonzales and he was first through the door.
But I was unzipped, let rip, zipped again and out before he could even draw.

Now God killed John Lennon and he let Barry Manilow survive,
But the good Lord blessed little Adrian Mitchell with the fastest cock alive.

A Ballad of Human Nature

The Buddha sat on a banana crate
Sunning his mind in the shade,
Trying to imagine Aggressive,
Trying to imagine Afraid.

A man staggered up to the Buddha,
He was horrified and thin.
He was hacking with a knife at his body,
Paring his own skin.

The Buddha said: 'Be kind to yourself.'
The thin man lowered his knife;
Then he said, as his blood ran into the earth:
'Where've you been all your life?

'You know, you can't change human nature just like that.
I once saw it proved in a book by a scientist's rat.
We're jellies shaking with atavistic greed.
You can't change human nature – you may as well bleed.'

This Friend

I've got this friend you see and it was the Cuba crisis and the voices were telling him that there was a plot to set the world on fire and so he shook his way round London lurching deliberately into policemen so they took him in and they knocked out his front teeth and all the time they were knocking out his front teeth they were calling him SIR and after he had been in Brixton for a week or maybe more he doesn't remember they decided he was mad.

This friend now carries a certificate which guarantees that he is schizophrenic.

Birthdays
(for Ray Charles)

You shout that you're drowning,
You give it everything.
A manager walks by and says:
'That little cat can sing.'
You go to bed mad
And you think that's bad
But what you going to do
When you wake up mad?
There'll be no more birthdays.

I'm talking about
Pain man and fear man and shock man and death man,
Not the Hollywood kind.
I'm talking about
Man made of bone made of wood made of stone
By some Frankenstein.
Talking about
Pain man and fear man and shock man and death man,
The crumbling mind.

There was this astronaut
And one day he found
He couldn't talk
Any more to the ground.
The instruments said
He was stuck for eighty years,
His helmet began
To fill up with tears –
And it was his BIRTHDAY.

I'm talking about
Pain man and fear man and shock man and death man,
Not the Hollywood kind.
I'm talking about
Man made of bone made of wood made of stone
By some Frankenstein.
Talking about
Pain man and fear man and shock man and death man
The crumbling mind.

The Only Electrical Crystal Ball I Ever Saw
Flickering Behind a Bar

What colour?
O the colour of an apple in love,
A tomfool tomato,
Changing its soft electric moods each second –
Intimate maps, galactic anatomical charts
Never to be repeated.
Well one moment it exploded with every brand of crimson,
The next it was awash with the blue of peace –
Ocean, pacific ocean –
Or became a green place swarmed over by dark canals.

I said to the man behind the bar:
Where does it come from?
He said: I made it myself.
I was so glad I laughed.
I said: Where is it going to?
He laughed.

Sunset over Venus in a goldfish bowl.
Silent jukebox with no money-slot
But pulsing with molten rainbows.
Belisha beacon drunkenly standing,
Head back, mouth open,
Under a hundred-foot-high colourfall
Of brandy soda crème de menthe
Sherry-spiked wine of the country
(Plus a secret formula)
Flowing from a vat with a fuller draught
Than the Tuscarora Deep.

This is no magic melon to solve all our dandruff
But a small machine for giving.
It added some light to my happiness.
It is a good planet.
I call it the earth.

Snaps

                              drinks brandy all the time
                              at his age
                              he deserves it

small dog slowly
waves her tail
at the sun

                              bad morning
                              the ceiling of his skull
                              has measles

those berserk lambs
suddenly apply the brakes
wrong mother

Funnyhouse of a Negro
(for Adrienne Kennedy)

A head
beating against a wall
A beautiful head
beating against a wall
The beautiful head of a woman
beating against a wall
The beautiful head of a woman with her wrists and ankles chained
beating against a wall

A million beautiful heads
beating against a wall

And the first brick is shaken loose
topples
and begins to fall

My Dog Eats Nuts Too
(CHEKHOV: *The Cherry Orchard*)

The sperm bank manager shoved me up against the rail
he levelled his gamma ray at my adventure tail
he said I've followed you through fire and flood and firkin
And you'd better explain just what you think you're working

I said:
I'm not a motivational expert you'd better suppose
but the trouble is my brain is a long way behind my nose
I believe in saluting the animals, my motto is dig and have done
but I spend all my problemofleisure grabbing lots of chinese fun

having chinese fun
having chinese fun
you don't need a mantelpiece
when you're having chinese fun

He said:
you're chewing something terrible, show us your expectoration
so I banged the spittoon with western civilisation
he clamped me with his grabbers and shook me till my steeple rung
tell me what's so special he said about chinese fun

having chinese fun
having chinese fun
happy as the hebrides
when I'm having chinese fun

I said:
it moves like a leopard on ice cubes
glows like hot molasses
its a shady bank by the old gulf stream
and there's masses and masses and masses for the masses
giggles every time that it tries to be sensible
striped with sex well it's highly reprehensible
but I'll bring you a cut of it only costs a dollar a ton
and you'll feel like a Zen Gun once you've tasted chinese fun

having chinese fun
having chinese fun
take the moon and rub it all over the surface of the sun
and you'll turn in your badge
when you've had some chinese fun

He tried it.
He liked it.
He said: thank you.

A Spell to Make a Good Time Last

Walk with your lover through a doorway
Walk with your lover through the maytime sunlight
Walk with your lover by a lake

The past is a stone for playing ducks and drakes
The stone is lying at your feet
Skim the stone away across the lake

The future is a stone for playing ducks and drakes
The stone is lying at your feet
Skim the stone away across the lake

Lie down beside the water
Lie down beside your lover
Lie down beside the water
Lie down beside your lover

A Spell to Make a Bad Hour Pass

Unfold your hand
Place all of the bad minutes in a circle
In the palm of your hand

Close your fingers slowly
To form a gentle fist

Slowly turn your fist around
And let your eyes pass slowly
Over all the surface of your fist

Slowly turn your fist around
And let your lips pass slowly
Over all the surface of your fist

Slowly
Tighten your fingers
Slowly
Tighten your fist

The fist is clenched
All the bad minutes are inside it
The fist is clenched
This evil hour is vanishing

Slowly slowly
Unfold the fingers of your hand

The palm of your hand is empty

Rest the back of your hand
Upon your other hand

Look into the palm of your hand
Look deep into your hand

Your hand is full
Your hand is full
Your hand is full of life

OUT OF THE VALLEY OF DEATH RODE THE 600000000...

A Curse on My Former Bank Manager

May your computer twitch every time it remembers money
until the twitches mount and become a mechanical ache
and may the ache increase until the tapes begin to scream
and may the pus of data burst from its metal skin

and just before the downpour of molten aluminium
may you be preening in front of your computer
and may you be saying to your favourite millionaire
yes it cost nine hundred thousand but it repays every penny

and may the hundred-mile tape which records my debts spring out
like a supersonic two-dimensional boa-constrictor
and may it slip under your faultless collar and surround your hairless neck
and may it tighten and tighten until it has repaid everything I owe you

A Song for Jerry Slattery and His Family

Here's your life, Jerry, they said, go out and spend it –
So he lumbered out into the world and saw that it was good
But could be a darn sight better, but he began to enjoy himself
After first making sure that everyone between him and the horizon
Had a drink in their hand and somebody to talk to...

Surgery: fifty monologues a day, nervous, desperate.
Listen. Advise. Listen. Refer. Listen. Sign a little note.
The troubles of others cascaded through his mind
While his round eyes said I understand yes I understand
As he cared, and comforted, and cured.

Then home to throw the same old wonderful party,
Greeting you by hallooing your name twice then what are you having,
Drawing you into the corner between fireplace and window
To let you in on a joke against the Tories
Or declare his worship for *The Balkan Trilogy* or the Cameron column.

A one-man scrum shoving boredom off the pitch and out through the turnstile.
A one-man Ireland swallowing his sorrows and sharing out his joys.
A one-man summertime for friends among whom he was famous,
He lives in all who loved him, and may we spend our lives
As generously as Jerry, as generously as Johnnie.

A Wedding Song for My Niece Ruth Mitchell and Her Husband Nigel Pickersgill

The very first baby that ever I met was my brother Jimmy now a professor
He was two years old I was aged nil and he seemed about the size of a Welsh
        dresser
I lay there blowing gripe-water bubbles and remarked that if it'd make him happy
I'd stick to the arts, he could have science – then he kicked me up the nappy

Years of fraternal feuding flew by, with battles only I and he know,
When I was an addict of *Dandy* and he was hooked on the *Beano*,
Till I became the teenager responsible for Esher Surrey Gents Inscriptions
While Jimmy was sent by King George the Six to pacify the Egyptians

And when he came back we liked each other, we were friends, even good friends
        maybe
But I still recalled his resemblance to Cain when he was a two-year-old baby
And my anti-infant prejudice induced me to prefer alligators
To the gurgling and talcumed menaces who inhabit perambulators

Then Jimmy met Anne, they married each other – coincidences never cease –
They were so fond of me they went out of their way to manufacture me a niece –
All my fear of babies folded away, for she was a heart-leaping sight
She fitted perfectly into my arms and her hair was bright as the light.

I worshipped the ground she wobbled upon but I was one of a congregation
Of dedicated Ruth worshippers in a circle of adoration
At four years old on my lap in a car she improvised a four-hour song
Which I nicked and stuck in a poem of mine (but I cut it to two minutes long)

Never more never more will she sit on my lap though now she is lovelier still
For Ruth, who makes angels look dowdy, is now Mrs Pickersgill.
To her and Nigel – laughter, joy, great happiness and peace
And please to supply a great nephew or preferably a great niece.

A Curse Against Intruders

(Written after the house of Cicely Smith, the poet, and Ian Herbert, the clarinettist, was robbed by a knife-wielding thug)

Burglar-bungler
Ransom-ransacker
Thug-unhugged-mugger
Orchestra attacker
You who tread maliciously
Into this good Herbertry

Your nerves shall be torn into raffia,
Done most debilitating, grievous harm
And this not through some magic Mafia
Roused by this spell's clanging alarm
But through a slow, gyrating, spiral curse
The which shall corkscrew up you, verse by verse,
Till you'll wish you rode your own hearse –
(I'll soon be hoarse, so I'll be terse) –
A mumping thumping curse and worse
Fall on your heart, that bulged-with-poison purse.

You, Scowler with the Knife, may gulp
Before you slash a clarinettist's hands.
Behind you a rock-wielding poet stands
Ready to crush you into dismal pulp.

Piss off! Piss off you fart-filled fool!
Your arteries I'll use for wool
And when I've plained them and I've purled
You'll be right knitted up, then hurled
Into the Dustbin of the Universe.
These are the best people in the world
And you had better never ever trouble them
Or I'll take your worst scares and double them
And I'll take your best hopes and rubble them.

Epithalamium for Maeve and Gordon Binchy-Snell

Economic communities for the directors of Octopoid Interplanetary
Urban environments for the planners of Boredom Lump City
Developmental hypermarkets for the franchiseholders of Colonel Doom Dog-Nuts
Low density population zones for the League of Poisoners in their Nuclear Castles
but an island for lovers

Ice-blue uniforms for the team of Aerobatic Millionaires
Grey for the ostrich-stepping Regiment of Bureaucrats
Black for the Secret and Blatant Police   Scarlet for the Daytime Butchers
The gold of turds for the crowns of the Mighty and Almighty.
but green for lovers

yes
a green island of love for Maeve and Gordon
a green island set in a guinness-foaming sea
a green island in a brilliant archipelago of friends
where jazz-enchanted pleasure steamers
packed with fun-booze, glow-books, jokeshop japes and Tibetan take-outs,
toot their greetings to the little painted paddle-boats
propelled by pedals pushed by cheerful feet

yes
Gordon and Maeve
may your future wave
like a wild patchwork flag in the good luck air
Maeve and Gordon
enjoy your garden
as bright as a Jack B. Yeats painted fair

My Parents

My father died the other day and I would like to write about him. Because I think of them together, this means also writing about my mother, who died several years ago.

About a thousand people called her Kay, most of them people she helped at some time, for she was what chintzy villains call a 'do-gooder'. Nobody ever called her that to her face or in my family's hearing; if they had, she'd have felt sorry for them. Both her brothers were killed in the First World War. She wore two poppies on Remembrance Day. She divided her life between loving her family, bullying or laughing innumerable committees into action rather than talk, giving, plotting happiness for other people, and keeping up an exuberant correspondence with several hundred friends.

She was not afraid of anyone. She was right. A Fabian near-pacifist, she encouraged me to argue, assuming right-wing positions sometimes so that I was forced to fight and win the discussion.

She tried to hoist the whole world on her shoulders. After each of her first two cancer operations, on her breasts, she seemed to clench her fists and double the energy with which she gave. She wasn't interested in unshared pleasure.

After the second operation she answered the door one day to a poor woman whom she didn't know. The woman asked where 'the wise woman' lived. My mother knew who she meant – a rich clairvoyant who lived down the road. Not trusting that particular witch, my mother asked what was wrong. The poor woman's doctor had told her that she must have a breast removed, and she was very scared. My mother said, but there's nothing to that, look – and she took out the two rolled socks which she kept in her empty brassière and threw them up into the sunlight and then caught them again. So the poor woman came in, drank tea, talked, forgot many fears, and went away knowing that she had seen the wise woman.

People called my father Jock. Face tanned from working in his garden, he survived the trenches of the First World War. He spoke very little. When he talked it was either very funny or very important. He only spoke to me about his war twice, and then briefly. In my teens I wrote a short, Owen-influenced poem about that war. My father read it, then told me of a friend who, during the lull between bombardments, fell to all fours, howled like an animal and was never cured.

Usually he avoided company. There was something in other people which frightened him. He was right. At the seaside he would sit on the farthest-out rock and fish peacefully. When visitors called at our house he would generally disappear into his jungle of raspberry canes and lurk.

Maybe there were twenty or thirty people in the world whose company he really enjoyed. They were lucky; he was a lovely man. Like Edward Lear, he was most at his ease with children, who instantly read, in the lines radiating from the corners of his eyes, that this was a man who understood their games and jokes.

He was short and lean and had fantastic sprouting Scottish eyebrows. He was a research chemist, but that didn't mean he only took an interest and pride in my elder brother's scientific work. He let me see how glad he was that I wrote, and I still remember the stories he used to write for me and my brother.

A year or so before he died he was in London for the day. My father sometimes voted Tory, sometimes Liberal, but when he began to talk about Vietnam that day, his face became first red and then white with anger about the cruelty and stupidity of the war. I seldom saw him angry and never so angry as at that moment, a man of seventy, not much interested in politics, all the grief of 1914-18 marching back into his mind.

People sometimes talk as if the ideological conflicts between generations have to be fought out bloodily, as if it is inevitable that children should grow to hate their parents. I don't believe this. Our family was lucky: my brother and I were always free to choose for ourselves – knowing that, however odd our decisions, we were trusted and loved. We all loved one another and this love was never shadowed.

Taming a Wild Garden
(for Celia, 5 April 1978)

I peck away with my pick-axe beak
To break the crust of builders' concrete
And let the ground of our garden breathe.

I rake away cream-coloured crumbs
And there's the brown earth
I never spend long enough learning from.
There's the brown earth
I never spent long enough loving.

My brown-faced tabby cruises by.
I bend to stroke her as she goes.

My chest warms.
My brown-faced father
Who loved his garden and several cats,
Smiles inside my heart.

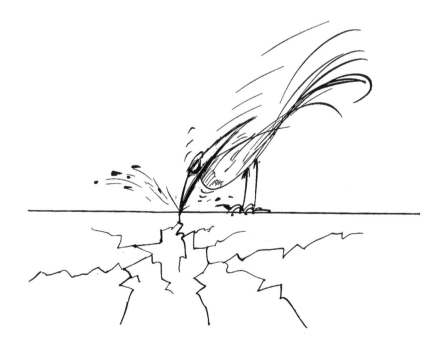

One More Customer Satisfied

He staggered through the cities moaning for melons:
'Green melons streaked with yellow!
Yellow melons tinged with green!
Don't try to fool me. They fooled me before
With tie-dyed green-and-yellow footballs
And the breasts of yellow women, green-tinted nipples...'

In his yellow rage and his green longing
He rolled himself into a melon-shaped heap of hopelessness
Crying out: 'Melons! Bring out your melons!'

So they took a million melons to Cape Kennedy,
Scooped them out, filled them with green and yellow paint
And splattered them all over the bright side of the moon.

They adjusted his face so it faced the face of the moon
And they told him: 'There is your one true melon,
Your forever melon, your melon of melons.'

Now, fully grateful, he watches the melon rise,
The setting of the melon, the new melon and the full melon,
With a smile like a slice of melon in the green-and-yellow melon-light.

Io, Io, It's off to Work We Go

To be seduced by a cloud
It's like wrestling with a weightless bear
He was all around me in and out of me
Whispering his small rain everywhere

Now I am an old walking woman
My skin is like yellow leather
But I keep half an eye cocked at the sky
And I smile when they talk about the weather

So when the sky gets randy to rain
I never run for cover
For a man is only a fool on a stick
But a cloud is a total lover

To My Friends, on My Fiftieth Birthday

My darlings, my friends, makers of all kinds, what can I say to them?
Go on with your labours of love, for you build Jerusalem.
My friends, my darlings, what can I say about you?
I will love you forever, I would have died without you.

How to Be Extremely Saintly, Rarefied and Moonly
(for Becky, who, when I spoke about resisting my urge to lie around watching videos all day told me: 'Let your temptation never fail you.')

Let your coconut be your guide
Let the sun stew in its own juice
Let your coat and rent your hat
And let your temptation never fail you

Let the good times roller-skate
Let me inside-out please, I forgot my keys
Let the flim-flam floogie with the floy-floy rock 'n' roll
But let your temptation never fail you

Let the lecturer be harangued by the blackboard
Let your letters stamp their footling feet to better letter music
Let us play soccer together with a bonny lettuce
And in the Beantime –
Let your temptation, Becky, never fail you.

Falling Feathers

(for Andy and Gill on their wedding day Saturday, 7 May 1983)

watch out for falling feathers
golden sailboats in the air
watch out for falling feathers
or they'll settle in your hair

    and you'll look pretty silly with golden feathers
    thrilling all over your nut
    you'll never get a mentionable pensionable job
    you'll live in a hut with a wooden water-butt

    you'll have to sidle round the countryside side-ways
    dancing to the music of bats
    attempting to make a magical living
    cutting rabbits in half producing girls out of hats

o watch out for falling feathers
golden rockinghorses in the air
watch out for falling feathers
or they'll settle in your hair

    and you'll be no better than your singing
    and no better than your audience too
    and you'll be no better than feathers falling
    golden golden down the blue

    and you'll be no better than hedgehogs
    who can only live like hedgehogs live
    and you'll be no better than the holy Jumblies
    who went to sea like you in a sieve

yes watch out for falling feathers
golden lions prowling down the air
watch out for falling feathers
or they'll settle in your hair

    ten miles overhead there's a couple of angels
    loving in a cloud on springs
    and they got a little archangelic
    and a couple of feathers jumped off of their wings

so live like a couple of featherheads
who got married on Uppendown Hill
for the feathers fell off a pair of angels
whose names coincidentally are Andy and Jill

watch out for falling feathers
golden cradles in the air
watch out for falling feathers
and catch them and save them
and take them and place them
golden in your children's hair

watch out for falling feathers
golden in the golden air
watch out for falling feathers
and they'll settle in your hair
in your happyeverafter hair

Loony Prunes

(an apology poem for my daughter)

We played the savage ludo which is known as Coppit,
Chatted, drank wine, ate lamb, played Beatle tunes
And then we started it, found we couldn't stop it –
A contest to eat maximum loony prunes.

They weren't just the ordinary, wrinkled, black,
Laxative fruit imported from – who knows?
But, floating in a stinging pool of Armagnac,
They were sozzled Français lunatic pruneaux.

Then, indoor fireworks, and the sharp flashes
Of three-second sparklers, dull horse-races,
A wonderful serpent, a frilly fern of ashes –
While the loony prune-juice flushed our faces.

As I was trying to put the fireworks out
We started arguing like sun and moon.
I grabbed you as the whole world seemed to shout.
You ran upstairs. I'm sorry. I'm a loony prune.

Sally Go Round the Ombelibus on a Thursday Afternoon
(for Sally Stephens)

First time I saw Sally
She was moving through the meadow
Lazing on her mother's lovely arm.

Together in the big marquee
She was just the right size for beauty
Held against my heart,
And I saw her daddy smile
A wider smile.

Milk was warm
Blue air was chilly
Trees and hedges
Danced circles round Sally
Green afternoon
Green afternoon
And my heart filled up again.

For Gordon Snell – My Best, First and Finest Friend
– on His Fiftieth Birthday

'By and by they all are dead' – stage direction at the end of an
early play by Gordon Snell, writer for grown-ups and children.
'By and by is easily said' – Hamlet in Hamlet, *a part once*
played by Gordon Snell.

By and by they all are dead –
The people, animals, earth and sky.
By and by is easily said.

Any child who has ever read
Knows that Book People cannot die.
By and by they all are dead?

Peter Rabbit's still raiding the potting shed
Under Long John Silver's laser eye.
By and by is easily said,

But Alice and the Golux tread
Emerald Oz where the Jumblies fly.
By and by they all are dead?

Lorna Doone and Just William wed
Where The Wild Things Are with Harriet the Spy.
By and by is easily said...

Gordon – the creatures your fancy has bred
Shall live with them – that's the sweet By-and-By!
By and by they all are dead?
By and by is easily said!

Shoot-out at the Hebden Bridge Saloon

(for Joy Smedley)

Pony Express rider
leaned down and muttered:
Watch out for the Gold-Dust Kid,
gonna be the fastest...
then he hit the horizon with his horse.

Waited awhile...
I'm takin a taste at the bar
when this gold-colour kid
kinda jumpy
but Apache eyes
moseys in, tosses a bag of dust on the bar –
Bourbon.

You the Gold-Dust Kid?

yup

Heard you're fast.

Yup.

Show me.

We locked eyes.
Made my move.

In through my ribs
out through my backbone.

Pour a last whiskey down me, Doc
And – watch out for the Gold-Dust Kid,
She...

For Nigel and Delyth

(Mumbles, June 1982)

Nightfall: the harp is playing like a fountain.
The harp is dancing like a happy woman.
The heartbeat of the house is the harp
As it sings like the spinning world.

Young Merlin splashes in the generous fountain.
He eats and drinks happiness with his woman
And the sea lies below them like a mighty harp
And his making table is a brown field in a new world.

Sardinia, 1979

(for Boty)

Yellow lampshine through the leaves of the tambourine.
Black waves of jelly slapping the white jetty.
Forty grandfathers sit round a Victorian tree.
Five of us are discussing our spaghetti.

To Michael Bell

(my teacher at Greenways School whose motto was:
'A Green Thought in a Green Shade')

In the second year of the Slaughter
I attended a school in Hell
Feeling like King Lear's fourth daughter
Strapped down in a torture cell
Then my blue and white mother appeared to me
And she saw I was all afraid
So I was transported mysteriously
To a green school in a green shade

And there I met a great mechanic
And he mended my twisted wings
And he gentled away my panic
And he showed me how a vision sings
And I thank Michael Bell most lovingly
For the mountains and lakes he made
And the way he shone the light of peace on me
Like a green thought in a green shade

Beattie Is Three

At the top of the stairs
I ask for her hand. O.K.
She gives it to me.
How her fist fits my palm,
A bunch of consolation.
We take our time
Down the steep carpetway
As I wish silently
That the stairs were endless.

Songs from
Some of the Shows

Gardening

(FROM *The Free Mud Fair at Totnes*)

EVE: At the heart of the Garden of Eden
       Lay a pool of golden mud

       I was the pool
       And my name was Eve
       One day I stood up like a fountain
       And began to mould my body
       Till it felt right and good

       Then I made Adam out of the same golden mud
       I made him different for fun

ADAM: Thank you for creating me

EVE: Shall we make more people out of mud?

ADAM: Yes
       You make some like me
       I'll make some like you

EVE: Let's make them all different

ADAM: Why make them different?

EVE: For fun for fun
       For fun for fun

ADAM: No... No...
       Two kinds is enough
       Two kinds is plenty

EVE *(to audience)*:
       My secret name is Peace
       (to ADAM*)*
       All right, Adam

EVE & ADAM:
       So we made children out of the mud
       Thousands of children out of the mud
       Two kinds of children
       Only two kinds
       All of them totally different

The Violent God
(FROM *Move Over, Jehovah*)

Barbed wire all around the Garden of Eden
Adam was conscripted for the First World War
And it's still going on, and it's still going strong –
Hail to the violent god.

The old survivor said: I was in Belsen,
I'm grateful to god because he got me out of Belsen,
When I die please bury me in Belsen –
Hail to the violent god.

The god of hunger eats the people of India
The god of law and order spends most of his time
Smiling at the back of torture rooms –
Hail to the violent god.

Children were smitten with parents.
The black man was smitten with the white man.
The white man was smitten with the motor car –
Hail to the violent god.

Spastics teach us how to have pity
Leukaemia teaches us the dangers of anarchy
Schizophrenia teaches us sanity –
Hail to the violent god.

The Hairy Men from the Hills
(FROM *Lash Me to the Mast!*)

We are the Hairy Men from the Hills
We deal very hairily with anyone who gums us up
We are the Hairy Men from the hills
And that about sums us up
We are the Hairy, very very Hairy
Hairy Men from the Hills

Calypso's Song to Ulysses
(FROM *Lash Me to the Mast!*)

My hands are tender feathers,
They can teach your body to soar.
My feet are two comedians
With jokes your flesh has never heard before.

So try to read the meaning
Of the blue veins under my skin
And feel my breasts like gentle wheels
Revolving from your thighs to your chin.

And listen to the rhythm
Of my heartbeat marking the pace
And see the visions sail across
The easy-riding waters of my face.

What is sweeter than the human body?
Two human bodies as they rise and fall.
What is sweeter than two loving bodies?
There is nothing sweeter at all.
Lose yourself, find yourself,
Lose yourself again
On the island of Calypso.

The Children of Blake
(FROM *Tyger Two*)

The children of Blake dance in their thousands
Over nursery meadows and through the sinister forests,
Beyond the spikes of cities, over the breasts of mountains,
The children of Blake dance in their thousands.
They dance beyond logic, they dance beyond science,
They are dancers, they are only dancers,
And every atom of their minds and their hearts and their deep skins
And every atom of their bowels and genitals and imaginations
Dances to the music of William Blake.

Happy Birthday William Blake

(FROM *Tyger Two*)

When he was alive everybody used to put him down.
Now they're writing volumes and they say they're sad he's not around.
But they wouldn't know Blake if they saw him
And heard him
And shook him by the hand.
They wouldn't know Blake if they took him
And tried him
And shot him from the witness stand.

For Blake was a man like any other man
But he trained his hands to see
And he trained his tongue to pop out of his ears
And he cried with his toenails
And the hairs in his nostrils
Danced to the music of the oxygen.

And they took a thousand million bricks
And they laid down Blake like a foundation stone
And they built a city-prison on his chest
But nothing could hold him down.

For he took a draught of explosive air
And he shook off London like a crust.
And he sang as he stood on the edge of the world
And he worked as he stood as he sang
And he built Jerusalem
He built Jerusalem
With his soft hard
Hard soft hands.

So it's happy birthday William Blake
What you've done can never be undone.
Happy birthday William Blake
Tyger of Jerusalem and Lamb of London.
Happy birthday happy birthday
Happy birthday William Blake.

Poetry

(FROM *Tyger Two*)

Poetry glues your soul together
Poetry wears dynamite shoes
Poetry is the spittle on the mirror
Poetry wears nothing but the blues

It's the gumboil gargoyle that falls off the cathedral
To land on the crown of the Queen.
Grab it while you can, it's the magical needle.
It's bitter sixteen and its flesh is bright green

Poetry glues your soul together
Poetry wears dynamite shoes
Poetry is the spittle on the mirror
Poetry wears nothing but the blues

Poetry's a lion on the stage of the opera house
Doin' a little jammin' with his brothers and sisters
Hits you, slits you, almost never fits you,
you and your lover get covered in blisters.

Poetry glues your soul together
Poetry wears dynamite shoes
Poetry is the spittle on the mirror
Poetry wears nothing but the blues

Poetry's the moon's own bottle of gin.
It's the purple ghost of Duke Ellington's band.
It's a bucket with a hole for collecting truth in
And the legless beggar army of Disneyland

Clinton hasn't got it, but there's plenty in Fidel.
Slap your sherry trifle on my sewing machine.
Bend it into bowlines but you'll never break it
The only way to make it is the way you make it
Only thing that matters is the way you shake it

Poetry glues your soul together
Poetry wears dynamite shoes
Poetry is the spittle on the mirror
Poetry wears nothing but the blues

The Tribe
(from *Man Friday*)

The tribe changes
As a tree changes.

When the storm throws its weight against a tree
The tree bends away.
When the storm falls asleep upon the tree
The tree stands up again.

The tribe changes
As a tree changes.

The children are the blossoms of the tree,
They laugh along its branches.
The old are the fruit of the tree,
They fall when they are ready to fall.

The tribe changes
As a tree changes.

Nobody tells the tree how it should grow.
Nobody knows what shape it will assume.
The tree decides the angle of its branches.
The tree decides when it is ready to die.

Ride the Nightmare

(FROM *The Hot Pot Saga*)

I was zooming round the Universe feeling like Desperate Dan
I was bombing them at random looking for Charlie Chan
I looked and saw a continent without a single man
Which they told me was Asia but it looked more like Aberfan *

So ride the nightmare
Jump upon its hairy back
Ride the nightmare
Ride until your mind goes black
It's the 21st century werewolf
21st century werewolf
21st century werewolf and it's coming this way

Well the charity lady wiped the diamonds from her eyes and said
'I've been saving all my money but the African dead stay dead
I'm sending them elastoplast and dunlopillo bread –
But they wrote me a letter saying: Send us guns instead'

So ride the nightmare
Jump upon its hairy back
Ride the nightmare
Ride until your mind goes black
It's the 21st century werewolf
21st century werewolf
21st century werewolf and it's coming this way

Well the rich white Englishman can easily ignore the rest
For the poor are just a bore and who can use the starving and oppressed?
They're burning while you tell yourself there's nothing you can do
When your turn comes they'll do just the same for you

So ride the nightmare
Jump upon its hairy back
Ride the nightmare
Ride until your mind goes black
It's the 21st century werewolf
21st century werewolf
21st century werewolf and it's coming this way...

* *This first verse was rewritten around 1986 and it now goes:*
I was zooming round the universe feeling like Sylvester Stallone
I was bombing them at random looking for Gadaffi's home
I saw a Royal baby in a cradle of silver lace
And I saw another baby with flies feeding out of his face...

The Weighing Machine

(FROM *A Seventh Man*)

You buy a weighing machine
The kind made for a ballroom
With rubber on the platform
For bare wet feet.

You wrap it up in paper
You hurry through the city
Until you reach the station
And choose your street

And you sit there on the pavement
With your weighing machine unwrapped and displayed.
And you cry out, you cry out, all day long:
Your weight! Your true weight!
Your weight! Your true weight!

A whole day crying:
Your weight! Your true weight!

By the end of the day
You might have the cash
To pay for a meal
For one.

A whole day crying: –
Your weight! Your true weight!

Bus Station

(FROM *A Seventh Man*)

Small town bus station
Mud and grass parking space
A mess of wooden huts

Small town bus station
In the air a cloud of sound
As journeys are explained

> There's always a wind in such places
> Grit and litter whirling around your feet
> You don't always cringe from the cold in such places –
> Sometimes you're flattened by the heat

Small town bus station
Migrants, soldiers, families
Who have to travel on

Small town bus station
The only thing you never see
Is anyone who's rich

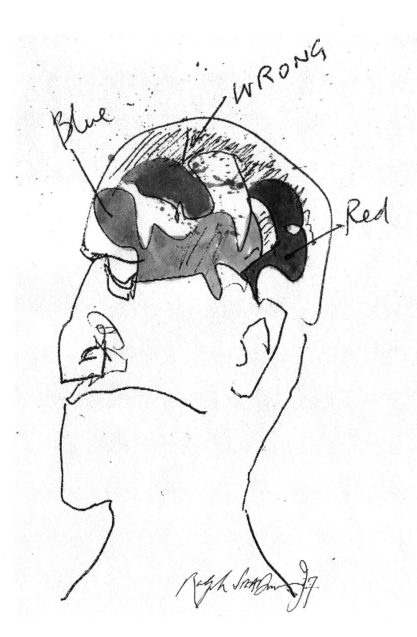

Medical
(from *A Seventh Man*)

The fit are being sorted out from the unfit.
One in five will fail.
Those who pass will enter a new life.
One in five will fail.

A Song of Liberation

(FROM *Houdini*)

Padlocked in a barrel full of beer
And almost dying from the fumes –
He did not despair.

Lashed to the waterwheel
Tied to the sail of a windmill –
His skill did not desert him.

Chained to the pillar of a prison cell
Riveted inside a metal boiler
Stuffed into the top of a roll-top desk
Sewn inside a giant sausage-skin –
He out-imagined every challenger.

Plunged into rivers, handcuffed and chained
Strapped to a crazy crib by mental nurses,
Tied to a cannon with a time fuse,
Hung upside down in the water torture cell,
In a Government mail pouch,
Even in the grave,
Even in the grave when he let himself be buried alive –

Even in the grave
His brain and body worked so perfectly
That he broke free from the grave.

And when the body of a man
Has been buried in the earth
And that body reaches up to the surface
That body reaches up towards the light,
Towards whatever shines –
Joy fills the people, magical joy.
Joy at the magic of his liberation,
Magic that touches the surface of your skin
With a magical shiver.
What is magic then?
What is magic? What is magic?
                     Beauty that takes you by surprise.

The First Journey
(FROM *Houdini*)

Once upon a time
Beyond the outer universe
On the far black meadows of nowhere
The human race assembled.
We made sure everyone was present and prepared.
Then we began our journey.

Under Niagaras of meteorites
Through jungle galaxies,
Over deserts of ammonia,
Along the million-year-deep canyons
Which gape between the stars,
We travelled together,
Towards the light,
Looking for a home.

On the planet Pluto
And on the planet Neptune
And on the planet Uranus
We froze in chemical oceans.
The sun no brighter than a match.
On the planet Saturn
The triple rings of silver
Dazzled and maddened us.

On the planet Jupiter
We were apples in the cider press
Of massive gravity.

On the planet Mars
We cried with thirst
And our tears were yellow dust.

On the planet Venus
We suffocated
Under four hundred miles
Of soaking clouds.

On the planet Mercury
We were offered
A choice of death by heat or cold.

But then we saw her
We saw our planet
Our earth
Our home

Let the people of the world
Shake off their chains and sing

There is no heaven but the Earth
There is no heaven but the People

Let the people of the world
Shake off their chains
And dance
And dance towards the light
Towards whatever shines.

Speedwell

(FROM *Houdini*)

The summit of the speedwell flower
Opens from green
Into an eye of blue and white
Staring towards the light,
Towards whatever shines.

A new-born baby's eyes
Turn towards the light,
Towards whatever shines.

A new-born baby's hands
Reach out towards the light,
Towards whatever shines.

The Widow's Song

(FROM *Mowgli's Jungle*)

My husband was strong
My husband was warm
His loving was
A thunderstorm
But a fever came
And took him by the hand
Now he is dancing,
Dancing, dancing
With the ghosts in Ghostland

My baby could stand
My baby could dance
His hands and legs
Like little plants
But a tiger came
And took him by the hand
Now he is dancing,
Dancing, dancing
With the ghosts in Ghostland

And now I am poor
As poor as a stone
All day and night
Alone alone
Let dreams tonight
Take me by the hand
And I'll go dancing,
Dancing, dancing
With the ghosts
With my lovely ghosts
With my lovely ghosts in Ghostland

The Truth

(FROM *Love Songs of World War Three*)

The truth is the truth
Is a strange kind of animal
The truth is the truth
Only comes out when people sleep
So I stay awake listening for the truth

    The truth's my favourite uncle
    Always brings me a surprise
    The truth's my favourite uncle
    What ridiculous stories it tells

I like the truth I like the way it doesn't simper
I like the truth it employs no PR men
I like the truth I'm very fond of its music
I like the truth I like the way it tastes
I like the truth it never gazes into mirrors
I like the truth I like its way of walking
I like the truth I'm very fond of its music
I like the truth I enjoy the way it tastes
I really love the truth

If it licks me I know it wants to lick me
If it leaves me I know it must be on its way

For the truth is the truth
Is a strange kind of animal
The truth is the truth
Only comes out when people sleep
So I stay awake listening for the truth

    It doesn't make hit records
    It's not often on the TV
    You'll see the truth more often
    In the sadness of faces on trains

I like its grin I like its way of falling silent
I like the way that it snoozes on committees
At soccer games it watches how the grass grows
It rents a shop and puts the worst in the window
I saw the truth in a junkyard one evening
I saw the truth it was sitting by a bonfire
I asked the truth, I said: What's your kind of music?
Tell you the truth, said truth, I like shining music
Yes I love the truth

For the truth is the truth
Is a strange kind of animal
The truth is the truth
Only comes out when people sleep
So I stay awake listening for the truth
Yes I stay awake listening for the truth

Wash Your Hands

(FROM *Mind Your Head*)

HUSBAND: My well-swept house is almost in the country
You can see woodlands from the upstairs window
On Saturday and Sunday there's a deck-chair on the patio
And there I drink a can or two of lager.

WIFE: Oh wash your hands, my darling,
Wash your hands, my darling,
Wash your clever hands.

HUSBAND: With my arm across my eyelids, I sleep very soundly.
My wife likes Chopin but I favour Mantovani.
My little girl of five goes to ballet class on Wednesday.
My little boy of seven collects toy vehicles.

WIFE: Oh wash your hands, my darling,
Wash your hands, my darling,
Wash your gentle hands.

HUSBAND: Every other weekend I take to my mother
A cake from the kitchen or flowers from the garden.
I always have a word and a wave for the neighbours
As I go to do the work which I never mention.

WIFE: Oh wash your hands, my darling,
Wash your hands, my darling,
Wash your loving hands.

HUSBAND: Sometimes I sit and stare at nothing
Sometimes I sit and smile at nothing
Sometimes I sit and think of nothing
My job is torturing men and women
My job is torturing men and women
My job is –

WIFE: Oh wash your hands, my darling,
         Wash your hands, my darling,
         Wash your shaking hands.

Marie Lloyd
(FROM *Mind Your Head*)

Marie Lloyd was warm as kettles
And as frank as celluloid
And her words could sting like nettles
Or caress like Marie Lloyd

    Marie Lloyd comes back and warm us
    Marie Lloyd return to us
    For your heart was as enormous
    As a double-decker bus

She had eyes like Dylan Thomas
And the wit of Nye Bevan
Marie Lloyd was taken from us
Send her back to succour man

    Marie Lloyd come back and warm us
    Marie Lloyd return to us
    For your heart was as enormous
    As a double-decker bus

Like a farted interruption
Of a speech by Sigmund Freud
Like Mount Etna in eruption
Is the heart of Marie Lloyd

    Marie Lloyd come back and warm us
    Marie Lloyd return to us
    For your heart is as enormous
    As a double decker bus

The Bum-Collector's Song
(FROM *Mind Your Head*)

Here I comes
With me bucket of bums
Isn't it a lovely day?

I live in the slums
With a posh set of drums
That I never have time to play

I've got double-jointed thumbs
And receding gums
But otherwise I'm OK

And when I meet my chums
Walking out with their mums
this is what I always say –

Here I comes
With me bucket of bums
Isn't it a lovely day?

Marry Your Mother
(FROM *Mind Your Head*)

M-A-Double R-Y
Your M-O-T-H-E-R.
Don't be shy
My little laddie,
She was good enough for Daddy.
Boom! Boom!
Back to the womb!
Where'd you get that Mum from?
Marry your Mother today
And go back where you come from!

Lament for the Jazz Makers

(FROM *We*)

As I was sitting all alone
Death called me on the telephone
I said – I'm sorry, I'm not free.
The fear of death is haunting me.

Death is the cop who can't be bought.
You always think you won't be caught,
Until you're busted, finally –
The fear of death is eating me.

Death grabs the young cat by the neck –
He stomped upon Bix Beiderbecke
Whose cornet rung so silvery.
The fear of death is shaking me.

And death has locked up Lester Young
And Billie Holiday who sung
Her beaten-up black poetry.
The fear of death is clutching me.

Tatum, Django, Charlie Mingus,
Death snapped off their cunning fingers
Like twigs from some old apple tree.
The fear of death is breaking me.

Death took the great Duke Ellington
And wore him down to skin and bone
For all his generosity.
The fear of death is taunting me.

Louis, Mama Yancey, Dinah,
Bessie Smith and Big Joe Turner
All work in death's bad factory.
The fear of death is chilling me.

He breathed in air, he breathed out light,
Charlie Parker was my delight
But Bird was cut down cruelly.
The fear of death is touching me.

And we must all of us go dwell
In Death's enormous Black Hotel.
At least we'll have good company –
The fear of death is killing me.

Gather Together

(FROM *We*)

Gather together
The snow-drinking waterfalls
Gather together
The tears of the pine
The glassy-winged insects
The woodpecker's drum

Gather together
The soft-springing forest floor
Gather together
The lumbering bear
Inflammable maples
The spears of the sun

Gather together
The cry of the falling tree
Gather together
The apple-green pond
The leap of the squirrel
The patience of stones

Gather together
The snaggle-toothed undergrowth
Gather together
The spite of the storm
The acrobat swallows
The glaring of bones

Gather together
The green-fountain conifers
Gather together
The choir of the wolves
The strong breath of mushrooms
The butterwort flowers

Gather together
The shouting of cataracts
Gather together
The racket of rooks
The songs of the forest
The forest is ours

The Pregnant Woman's Song
(FROM *The Blue*)

I am an ocean
And in my deeps
There is a baby curled
I am an ocean
And in my deeps
I keep a little world

My heart is strong
Strong as the burning sun at noon
My baby's heart is clear
Simple and light as the floating moon

Yes I am an ocean
And in my deeps
There is a baby curled
I am an ocean
And in my deeps
I keep a little world

Jake's Amazing Suit
(FROM *Silent Chorus*)

When you see me in my suit –
You'll look and at first
All you'll see is a burst
Of shimmering electric blue.
Then you'll focus in and see
That the vision is me
And I'm walking
And my suit is walking too

When you see me in my suit –
Flowing soft as milk
It'll be Thailand silk
That follows any move at all.
And its cut and its drape
Will lay on me a shape
Like I'm standing
Underneath a waterfall.

When you see me in my suit –
    I won't be able to walk out in public
    Because of my wonderful threads
    Never mind, instead
    We'll spend our life in bed
    With nothing but love in our heads
When you see me in my suit!

I once saw Miles Davis
Walk across the tarmac from an aeroplane.
Yes I once saw Miles Davis walking
Oh now let me explain –

His face was carved from a living mahogany tree-trunk.
He wore power sunglasses over his eyes
With silver pistons connected to his ears.
His beret sat on the top of his head
Like a little powder-blue cloud
And when he smiled it turned you to stone.
His suit was four-and-a-half times too big for his body.
It was kind of a tweed woven out of mountain light.
It had criss-cross lines of the sort of luminous
Green you only see on the top of birthday cakes.
And the luminous green lines
Criss-crossed over a meadow of bright creamy white

I once saw Miles Davis
Walk across the tarmac from an aeroplane
Yes I once saw Miles Davis walking
I can explain –

I want a suit like that
I want a suit like that
I want a suit so electric
If I leave it alone
It'll jump off the hanger
Take a walk on its own
Give me a suit like that
Give me a suit like that

So that my love will love me
Even more than she loves me
When she sees me in my suit
When she sees me in my suit.

Another Peaceful Day

(FROM *The Siege*)

High above the city of Arden
The hill is misty and steep
In the yellow sun of the morning
It looks like a lion asleep

All the hillside pathways are zig-zag
It's easy losing your way
But we will climb up to our orchard
To witness the blossoms of May

Sitting round a table under pink and white trees
Eating very slowly, enjoying each bite,
Sitting round a table with our memories,
Terrible and happy, from morning till night
Sitting round a table under pink and white trees
On a hill above the city of Arden

Sitting round and arguing the rights and the wrongs
Pass the roly-poly Let's have some more cheese
Harmonising sweetly on our favourite songs
Drinking wine together, the pink and the white –
Sitting round a table under pink and white trees
On a hill above the city of Arden

Another peaceful day
Feels like another peaceful day
And our troubles float away
And it's another peaceful day
On a hill above the city of Arden

You Got Twins

(FROM *The Siege*)

You got twins
You got trouble
You got twins
Got it double
You got a Cantona kick in your shins – *ooh* –
You got twins

You got twins
You got Babel
Like you're hit
With a table
And you're jumping right out of your skins – *ooh* –
You got twins

Twice as nice
If you like the squash
When you're up against the wall
And under the cosh
Twice as nice
Like getting stuck in your zipper
On the chopping block
Done up like a kipper

You got twins
No more quiet
You got twins
You got riot
You got a Vinny Jones grinding your bones – *ooh* –
You got twins

You got twins
Call for mammy
Here they come
Double-whammy
And that's how the mayhem begins – *ooh* –
It's the twins

Singleton kids
Are well pathetic
But twins are megacool
Copasetic
Twins were born
To be bitchin twitchin
If you can't stand the heat
Get out of the kitchen

You got twins
Got a punch up
You got twins
Bring your lunch up
You're surely gonna pay for your sins – *ooh* –
To the twins

You got twins
You got madness
You got twice
Times the badness
Have your skeleton collected in bins – *ooh* –
By the twins

Twice as hard
As a security guard
Or the pitbull lurking
In a builder's yard
Twice as nice
When you know how it feels
In a suit of armour full
Of electric eels

You got twins
You trouble
You got twins
Got it double
You'll find there's only two people who wins – *ooh* –
That's the twins!

Cardboard Rowing Boat

(FROM *The Siege*)

All I know
Is that when I go
I will stand beside an unknown sea
And that's why I ask my best friends
When I die won't you make for me –

A cardboard rowing boat
For my coffin
Painted in greens and blues
And dress me up in my
Faded denim
And my favourite running shoes
In my green and blue
Cardboard rowing boat

The poems of Blake in my
Left hand pocket
Navy rum in my right
And in my hand put an eating apple
And bury me late at night
In my green and blue
Cardboard rowing boat

And I'll row away
Cross that starry sea
Singing and drifting with the tide
And I'll row away
And maybe I'll meet you at the other side
In my green and blue
Cardboard rowing boat

OUR BLUE PLANET

The Castaways *or* Vote For Caliban

The Pacific Ocean –
A blue demi-globe.
Islands like punctuation marks.

A cruising airliner,
Passengers unwrapping pats of butter.
A hurricane arises,
Tosses the plane into the sea.

Five of them, flung on to an island beach,
Survived.
Tom the reporter.
Susan the botanist.
Jim the high-jump champion.
Bill the carpenter.
Mary the eccentric widow.

Tom the reporter sniffed out a stream of drinkable water.
Susan the botanist identified a banana tree.
Jim the high-jump champion jumped up and down and gave them each a bunch.
Bill the carpenter knocked up a table for their banana supper.
Mary the eccentric widow buried the banana skins,
But only after they had asked her twice.
They all gathered sticks and lit a fire.
There was an incredible sunset.

Next morning they held a committee meeting.
Tom, Susan, Jim and Bill
Voted to make the best of things.
Mary, the eccentric widow, abstained.

Tom the reporter killed several dozen wild pigs.
He tanned their skins into parchment
And printed the *Island News* with the ink of squids.

Susan the botanist developed new strains of banana
Which tasted of chocolate, beefsteak, peanut butter,
Chicken and bootpolish.

Jim the high-jump champion organised organised games
Which he always won easily.

Bill the carpenter constructed a wooden water wheel
And converted the water's energy into electricity.
Using iron ore from the hills, he constructed lampposts.

They all worried about Mary, the eccentric widow,
Her lack of confidence and her –
But there wasn't time to coddle her.

The volcano erupted, but they dug a trench
And diverted the lava into the sea
Where it formed a spectacular pier.
They were attacked by pirates but defeated them
With bamboo bazookas firing
Sea-urchins packed with home-made nitro-glycerine.
They gave the cannibals a dose of their own medicine
And survived an earthquake thanks to their skill in jumping.

Tom had been a court reporter
So he became the magistrate and solved disputes.
Susan the Botanist established
A university which also served as a museum.
Jim the high-jump champion
Was put in charge of law-enforcement –
Jumped on them when they were bad.
Bill the carpenter built himself a church,
Preached there every Sunday.

But Mary the eccentric widow...
Each evening she wandered down the island's main street,
Past the Stock Exchange, the Houses of Parliament,
The prison and the arsenal.
Past the Prospero Souvenir Shop,
Past the Robert Louis Stevenson Movie Studios,
Past the Daniel Defoe Motel
She nervously wandered and sat on the end of the pier of lava,

Breathing heavily,
As if at a loss,
As if at a lover,
She opened her eyes wide
To the usual incredible sunset.

Quit Stalling, Call in Stalin

I've got a system
A system a system
I've got a system
And everyone's going to fit in

The white folk the black folk
The brown folk the yellow folk
The men folk the women folk
Yes everyone's going to fit in

And if you don't fit my system
My system my system
If you don't fit my system
There's something the matter with you

You'll be locked up in a hospital
Hospital hospital
Locked up in a hospital
With thousands of others like you

Locked up with the misfits
Misfits misfits
Locked up with the misfits
You're going to be there till you die

But I'll be out in the system
The system the system
Working within the system
Having the time of my life

Two Good Things

there's one good thing about a cow-pat:
if you leave it in the sun it dries.
and there's one good thing about capitalism –
it dies.

All the World's Beauty

all the world's
beauty

salmon-leaping
up and over all
the huge chill wall
of the waterfall
where hurtling water
sprays and foams on the deep
and deepening dip
in the limestone's mouth
and on the limestone's lip

all the world's
beauty

yes i saw it all
like a washed ghost
out of the comer
of my timid eye

all the world's
beauty

but no i couldn't turn
myself around to bask in it –
i knew my duty:
to watch black tarmac miles of motorway
for the columns of the killers
willing themselves along to kill

all the world's
beauty

Remember Suez?

England, unlike junior nations,
Wears officers' long combinations.
So no embarrassment was felt
By the Church, the Government or the Crown.
But I saw the Thames like a grubby old belt
And England's trousers falling down.

Written During the Night Waiting for the Dawn

Let's unplug the radiotelescope.
Pablo Neruda, that abundant planet,
Has been eradicated from the Southern starscape.

Down at the market every stall's been stricken –
Withered tomatoes, warty pomegranates,
Dud wine, black milk and a two-headed chicken.

Shall we cheer ourselves up with a stroll by the river?
But the pebbles are undergoing classification,
The waterfall's levelled, the green banks paved over.

He loved his food, the people and the alphabet.
But now Chile, his bride, is under interrogation.
The electrodes have been placed. The sun has set.

Briefing

He may be fanatical, he may have a madness.
Either way, move carefully.
He must be surrounded, but he's contagious.

One of you will befriend his family.
One male and one female will love the subject
Until he loves you back. Gradually

Our team will abstract and collect
His mail, nail-clippings, garbage, friends, words, schemes,
Graphs of his fears, scars, sex and intellect.

Steam open his heart. Tap his dreams.
Learn him inside and inside out.
When he laughs, laugh. Scream when he screams.

He will scream. 'Innocent!' He'll shout
Until his mouth is broken with stones.
We use stones. We take him out

To a valley full of stones.
He stands against a shed. He stands on stones
Naked. The initial stones

Shower the iron shed. Those stones
Outline the subject. When he cries for stones
The clanging ceases. Then we give him stones,

Filling his universe with stones.
Stones – his atoms turn to stones
And he becomes a stone buried in stones.

A final tip. Then you may go.
Note the half-hearted stoners and watch how
Your own arm throws. And watch how I throw.

Ballade of Beans

Nightmare. A silver butcher's truck
Hurtles around my brain and chop
Goes the neck-chopper. Wake. I suck
Pus from my gums, then slowly prop
Bones till they stand upright. I slop
Water which last night rinsed our greens
Over my face. My coiled guts hop –
The sink is clogged with dead beans.

Truth will lie, panting, for a buck.
Philosophy's a lollipop.
Who heeds Religion's biddy cluck
Or cares when Justice goes flip-flop?
So U.N.O.'s a headless mop,
Peace never reached her early teens,
Terror's capsuled in each raindrop –
The sink is clogged with dead beans.

Switzerland's had a lot of luck,
But Cuba slugged a wealthy cop
And Europe stands where lightning struck
Twice lately. Berlin. Will it drop?
Will the earth's ice-protected top
Flip off to show dead submarines?
The world, the grubby old death shop,
The sink is clogged with dead beans.

Wilson, we're both about to stop
England tots up as England gleans
The grains of your crapulous crop –
The sink is clogged with dead beans.

From Rich Uneasy America to My Friend Christopher Logue

'Never again that sick feeling when the toilet overflows.'
ADVERTISEMENT: THE IOWA CITY PRESS-CITIZEN

Jim Hall's guitar walking around
As if the Half Note's wooden floor
Grew blue flowers and each flower
Drank from affluent meadow ground.
The lush in the corner dropped his sorrowing
When he noticed his hands and elbows dancing.
Long silver trucks made lightning past the window.
A two-foot hunter watch hung from the ceiling.
Then you prowled in. The guitar splintered,
The lush held hands with himself, trucks concertinaed.
The watch-hands shook between Too Late and Now.

As I sit easy in the centre
Of the U.S. of America,
Seduced by cheeseburgers, feeling strong
When bourbon licks my lips and tongue,
Ears stopped with jazz or both my eyes
Full of Mid-Western butterflies,
You drive out of a supermarket
With petrol bombs in a family packet
And broadcast down your sickened nose:
'It overflows. By Christ, it overflows.'

Official Announcement

    Her Majesty's Government has noted with regret
That seven unidentified flying objects are zooming towards the earth.
    Her Majesty's Government has noted with regret
That they look like angels except that their skins and their wings are as raw as
afterbirth.
    Her Majesty's Government has noted with regret
That our military computers wrote a billion-word message explaining why
they all chose suicide

258

Her Majesty's Government has noted with regret

That here come the angels, and each of the angels has a jar with an oceanful of plague inside.

Her Majesty's Government has noted with regret

That the first angel has poured out his jar and that British nationals and others who have the mark of the beast or have at some time in the past worshipped the image of the beast are being afflicted with sores so noisome and grievous that their bodies are flashing like pinball machines.

Her Majesty's Government has noted with regret

That the second angel has poured out his jar and that the sea has become as the blood of a dead man and that everything in the sea is dying including Her Majesty's submarines.

Her Majesty's Government has noted with regret

That the third angel has poured out his jar and that the Thames has become an enormous and open and pulsing jugular vein.

Her Majesty's Government has noted with regret

That the fourth angel has poured out his jar and that the heat of the sun has become amplified but a spokesman for Civil Defence advises John Bull to stick his head in a sandbag full of ice in order to postpone or avert the frying of his brain.

Her Majesty's Government has noted with regret

That the fifth angel has de-jarred and that – It's all gone dark, we can't see – and all citizens who do not bear an official seal of redemption are gnawing their tongues in pain.

Her Majesty's Government has noted with regret

That the sixth angel – Frog Devils! Unclean! Frog-Beast Armageddon!

Her Majesty's Government has noted with regret

That the seventh angel – IT IS DONE – voices thunder lightnings great earthquake such as such as was not since men were upon the earth, so mighty an earthquake and so great and every island including us every island is flying away and regretfully the mountains cannot be found and a great hail is falling with steel rain and fire that is wet.

All of which things, although we understand the provocation under which heaven is acting and take this opportunity of reaffirming our unshaken trust in the general principles and policies of heaven, and in the firm belief that all possible steps have been taken to ensure minimal civilian casualties and compassionate underkill –

Her Majesty's Government has noted with regret.

Let Me Tell You the Third World War Is Going to Separate the Men from the Boys

SON: Make sure the black blind fits the window,
          Don't let the light fly out.
          Where is the war tonight?

FATHER: No, this is peacetime.
          You are safely tucked up in England.
          Sleep tight, happy dreams.

SON: Listen, Daddy, are they ours or theirs?

FATHER: They are owls, they are nobody's
          Responsibility. This is peace.

SON: Today I lost a battle.
          I feel like mud.

FATHER: Snuggle down, snuggle down,
          Tomorrow you will win two battles.

SON: Yes, and I will feel like mud.

FATHER: Grow up, this is self-pitying hyper-bollocks.
          Nobody is really, actually trying to
          Literally kill us.

SON: Yes they are, Daddy,
          Yes they are

Programme for an Emergency

The world's population statistically,
Could stand together on the Isle of Wight
Shoulder to shoulder to shoulder.
There they could stand and watch the sea,
Sleeping in shifts by day and night,
Gracelessly growing older.

But Holland's son would rape Ireland's daughter
Or China's grandfather fall in the water.
Ozone would mingle with the scent of slaughter.

Still, England seems the most suitable site,
For here we are proud not to laugh or weep
And one gulp of the air will freeze the strongest man in sleep.

Naming the Dead

And now the super-powers, who have been cheerfully doubling their money by flogging arms wherever the price is right, put on their Sunday cassocks and preach peace to the Middle East. From their lips the word sounds like a fart. On *Twenty-Four Hours* the other night, Kenneth Allsop interviewed a British arms merchant who has been selling to both Egypt and Israel. Admitting that he was having some doubts about his trade (he is now on the verge of an ill-earned retirement) he said that nevertheless the real question was: Am I my brother's keeper? and that the answer was No. The question was of course first put by Cain, whose flag flies high over most of the major cities of the world.

The more abstract war is made to seem, the more attractive it becomes. The advance of an army as represented by dynamic arrows swooping across the map can raise the same thrill as a child gets from playing draughts. Dubious score-sheets which say how many planes the government would have liked to have shot down only add to the game-like quality of news – you tot up the columns and kid yourself that someone is winning.

Wartime governments sometimes allow this process to be taken a step nearer reality by issuing photographs of one atrociously wounded soldier (our side) being lovingly nursed by his comrades, and another picture of dozens of prisoners (their side) being handed cups of water (see under Sir Philip Sidney, gallantry of). Such poses represent a caricature of war's effect on human beings.

What have Arabs been doing? Killing Jews.

What have the Jews been doing? Killing Arabs.

Even that doesn't get us far in the direction of reality. To add statistics saying how many were killed takes us only an inch nearer.

Who is killed? What were they like? I would like to see every government in the world held accountable to the United Nations for every human being it kills, either in war or in peace. I don't just mean a statistic published in a secret report. I mean that all the newspapers of the country responsible should carry the name of the person killed, his photograph, address, number of his dependants and the reason why he was killed. (We often do as much for the victims of plane crashes.)

This would mean that in some countries the press would be swamped with death reports and even mammoth death supplements. (Well, what about the advertisers?) But I want more.

I would like every death inflicted by any government to be the subject of a book published at the state's expense. Each book would give an exhaustive biography of the corpse and would be illustrated by photographs from his family album if any, pictures he painted as a child and film stills of his last hours. In the back cover would be a long-playing disc of the victim talking to his friends, singing, talking to his wife and children and interviewed by the men who killed him.

The text would examine his life, his tastes and interests, faults and virtues, without trying to make him any more, villainous or heroic than he was. It would be prepared by a team of writers appointed by the United Nations. The final chapter would record the explanations of the government which killed him and a detailed account of the manner of his death, the amount of bleeding, the extent of burns, the decibel count of screams, the amount of time it took to die and the names of the men who killed him.

One book for every killing. I realise that this would take some planning. Each soldier would have to be accompanied by an interviewing, camera and research team in order to record the details of any necessary victim.

Most factories would turn out printing presses, most graduates would automatically become biographers of the dead. Bombing could only take place after individual examination of every person to be bombed. The cost of killing would be raised to such a pitch that the smallest war would lead to bankruptcy and only the most merciful revolution could be afforded. Hit squarely in the exchequer – the only place where they feel emotion – chauvinist governments might be able to imagine for the first time, the true magnitude of the obscenity which they mass-produce.

This is no bloody whimsy. I want a real reason for every killing.

Fifteen Million Plastic Bags

I was walking in a government warehouse
Where the daylight never goes.
I saw fifteen million plastic bags
Hanging in a thousand rows.

Five million bags were six feet long
Five million were five foot five
Five million were stamped with Mickey Mouse
And they came in a smaller size.

Were they for guns or uniforms
Or a dirty kind of party game?
Then I saw each bag had a number
And every bag bore a name.

And five million bags were six feet long
Five million were five foot five
Five million were stamped with Mickey Mouse
And they came in a smaller size

So I've taken my bag from the hanger
And I've pulled it over my head
And I'll wait for the priest to zip it
So the radiation won't spread

Now five million bags are six feet long
Five million are five foot five
Five million are stamped with Mickey Mouse
And they come in a smaller size.

Lord Home the Foreign Secretary

Lord Home, Lord Home has an oblong face
Not beautifully designed and not plug-ugly
But bland, bland, a mirror of the times.
And Lord Home's bland and oblong face
Comes from a long line of bland and oblong faces.
Well-bred, says his tailor, wielding a cunning pair of scissors
Expensively for Lord Home, who was expensive to cultivate.
Now the money has been spent irretrievably,
Lord Home has been educated, brought forward, inspected, approved,
The worthy product of a long line
Of worthy products.

Lord Home, Lord Home, began to open
The mouth in his oblong face.
His mouth began to open and it continued opening until it was half-open,
    quite open, wide open –
A clean chlorophylled cavern suitable for conversion into a shelter.
From the cavern crawled words in English which said the English love Berlin,
You remember that city when its forelock was black a swastika at the centre of
    each eyeball, that city when each large eye wept rubble and the bodies of
    people Jewish and Gentile.
He said that for love of that city the British are prepared to be blown into
    atomic dust,
But, he said, remember, he said but he said but, but he said, but –
They would rather not.

Lord Home, Lord Home is a coward, a man without the guts of a chicken.
Unworthy of the line of oblong, dusty faces.
For I want to be dust, to be democracy-loving free-enterprise dust.
Every damp atom in my body cries for dessication.
After the blast and the firestorm all my British atoms
Will patriotically assemble on the site where my heart once stood
To form a small malicious cloud.
After the blast and after the firestorm
This army of atoms which once I used for living
Will wait in mindless patience for an easterly wind
To carry the cloud over the pelmets of the iron curtain
To rain steadily down on Moscow,
Maiming the bad men, the bad women and the bad children of Russia.

Order Me a Transparent Coffin and Dig My Crazy Grave

After the next war…and the sky
Heaves with contaminated rain.
End to end our bodies lie
Round the world and back again.

Now from their concrete suites below
Statesmen demurely emanate,
And down the line of millions go
To see the people lie in state.

Nikita Ikes, Franco de Gaulles,
Officiate and dig the holes.
Mao tse-Sheks, Macadenauers,
Toting artificial flowers.

As they pay tribute each one wishes
The rain was less like tears, less hot, less thick.
They mutter, wise as blind white fishes,
Occasionally they are sick.

But I drily grin from my perspex coffin
As they trudge till they melt into the wet,
And I say: Keep on walking, keep on walking,
You bastards, you've got a hell of a way to walk yet.

A Child Is Singing

A child is singing
And nobody listening
But the child who is singing:

Bulldozers grab the earth and shower it.
The house is on fire.
Gardeners wet the earth and flower it.
The house is on fire,
The houses are on fire.
Fetch the fire engine, the fire engine's on fire.

We will have to hide in a hole.
We will burn slow like coal.
All the people are on fire.

And a child is singing
And nobody listening
But the child who is singing.

The Dust

Singing, as she always must,
Like the kitten-drowner with a howling sack,
Open-eyed through the shallow dust
Goes the dust-coloured girl with a child on her back.

A schoolgirl in a flowered dress,
Swayed by the swaying of a tree
And the sun's grin, in front of her family
One day became a prophetess.

Like a singer who forgets her song
She awkwardly leant from the graceful chair,
Balanced her fists in the drawing-room air
And said that everyone was wrong, that she was wrong.

Shocked by this infantile mistake
Her uncles and aunts were sad to find
This ugly girl with an ugly mind
In a house as rich as birthday cake.

When the bombs fell, she was sitting with her man,
Straight and white in the family pew.
While in her the bud of a child grew
The city crumbled, the deaths began.

Now, singing as she always must,
A refugee from a love burned black,
Open-eyed through the rising dust
Goes the dust-coloured girl with a child on her back.

Veteran with a Head Wound

Nothing to show for it at first
But dreams and shivering, a few mistakes,
Shapes lounged around his mind chatting of murder,
Telling interminable jokes,
Watching like tourists for Vesuvius to burst.

He started listening. Too engrossed to think,
He let his body move in jerks,
Talked just to prove himself alive, grew thin,
Lost five jobs in eleven weeks,
Then started drinking, blamed it on the drink.

He'd seen a woman, belly tattered, run
Her last yards. He had seen a fat
Friend roll in flames, as if his blood were paraffin,
And herded enemies waiting to be shot
Stand looking straight into the sun.

They couldn't let him rot in the heat
In the corner of England like a garden chair.
A handy-man will take a weathered chair.
Smooth it, lay on a glowing layer
Of pain and tie a cushion to the seat.

They did all anyone could do –
Tried to grate off the colour of his trouble,
Brighten him up a bit. His rare
Visitors found him still uncomfortable.
The old crimson paint showed through.

Each night he heard from the back of his head,
As he was learning to sleep again,
Funny or terrible voices tell
Or ask him how their deaths began.
These are the broadcasts of the dead.

One voice became a plaintive bore.
It could only remember the grain and shine
Of a wooden floor, the forest smell
Of its fine surface. The voice rasped on
For hours about that pretty floor...

'If I could make that floor again,'
The voice insisted, over and over,
'The floor on which I died,' it said,
'Then I could stand on it for ever
Letting the scent of polish lap my brain.'

He became Boswell to the dead.
In cruel script their deaths are written.
Generously they are fed
In that compound for the forgotten,
His crowded, welcoming head.

The doctors had seen grimmer cases.
They found his eyes were one-way mirrors,
So they could easily look in
While he could only see his terrors,
Reflections of those shuttered faces.

Stepping as far back as I dare
(For the man may stagger and be broken
Like a bombed factory or hospital),
I see his uniform is woven
Of blood, bone, flesh and hair.

Populated by the simple dead,
This soldier, in his happy dreams,
Is killed before he kills at all.
Bad tenant that he is, I give him room;
He is the weeper in my head.

Since London's next bomb will tear
Her body in its final rape,
New York and Moscow's ashes look the same
And Europe go down like a battleship,
Why should one soldier make me care?

Ignore him or grant him a moment's sadness.
He walks the burning tarmac road
To the asylum built with bricks of flame.
Abandon him and you must make your own
House of incinerating madness.

The horizon is only paces away.
We walk an alley through a dark,
Criminal city. None can pass.
We would have to make love, fight or speak
If we met someone travelling the other way.

A tree finds its proportions without aid.
Dogs are not tutored to be fond.
Penny-size frogs traverse the grass
To the civilisation of a pond.
Grass withers yearly, is re-made.

Trees become crosses because man is born.
Dogs may be taught to shrink from any hand.
Dead frogs instruct the scientist;
Spread clouds of poison in the pond –
You kill their floating globes of spawn.

In London, where the trees are lean,
The banners of the grass are raised.
Grass feeds the butcher and the beast,
But we could conjure down a blaze
Would scour the world of the colour green.

For look, though the human soul is tough,
Our state scratches itself in bed
And a thousand are pierced by its fingernails.
It combs its hair, a thousand good and bad
Fall away like discs of dandruff.

For a moment it closes its careful fist
And, keening for the world of streets,
More sons of god whisper in jails
Where the unloved the unloved meet.
The days close round them like a dirty mist.

When death covers England with a sheet
Of red and silver fire, who'll mourn the state,
Though some will live and some bear children
And some of the children born in hate
May be both lovely and complete?

Try to distract this soldier's mind
From his distraction. Under the powdered buildings
He lies alive, still shouting,
With his brothers and sisters and perhaps his children,
While we bury all the dead people we can find.

Life on the Overkill Escalator

Dogs must be carried because they do not understand.
You examine the shoulders of the man ahead without understanding.

You pass foreign-faced women. They pass you.
They are cardboard, behind glass. They wear lead corsets anyway.

The vibration becomes part of you
Or you become part of the vibration.

The penalty for stopping the escalator is five pounds.
Five pounds is a lot of money.

You Get Used to It

'Am I in Alabama or am I in hell?'
A MINISTER, MONTGOMERY, ALABAMA, MARCH 1965

Begging-bowl eyes, begging-bowl eyes,
skin round hoops of wire.
They do not eat, they are being eaten,
saw them in the papers.

   But it's only bad if you know it's bad,
   fish don't want the sky.
   If you've spent all your life in hell or Alabama
   you get used to it.

Ignorant husband, ignorant wife,
each afraid of the other one's bomb.
He spends all he has in the Gentlemen's
on a fifty p book of nudes.

   But it's only bad if you know it's bad,
   fish don't want the sky.
   If you've spent all your life in hell or Alabama
   you get used to it.

Beautiful blossom of napalm
sprouting from the jungle,
bloom full of shrivelling things,
might be mosquitoes, might be men.

But it's only bad if you know it's bad,
fish don't want the sky.
If you've spent all your life in hell or Alabama
you get used to it.

I hurt, you hurt, he hurts, she hurts,
we hurt, you hurt, they hurt.
What can't be cured must go to jail,
what can't be jailed must die.

But it's only bad if you know it's bad,
fish don't want the sky.
If you've spent all your life in hell or Alabama
you get used to it.

Two Dances

the clouds dance
to the split-second
finger-drumming
of the winds

the mountain dances
to the deep beat
of century
after century

different tempos
all one music

Good Question

How can the rich hate the poor?
They never see them.

Their chauffeurs swerve well clear of slums.
Accountants keep them out of jail.
Poor people do not run the BBC
So the rich never see the poor.

How can the poor hate the rich
When the rich are so pretty?

A chained man knows the weight of his chains.
A woman in jail has a strong sense of time.
Hunger is a wonderful schoolmaster.
The poor crouch. The poor watch. The poor wait.
The poor get ready. The poor will stand up.

How do the poor hate the rich?
Like a bullet.

Dumb Thursday

Ophelia watches the skating party
From her table in the Café Posthumous.
Landladies punch each other's rumps
In the belfry of Saint Machine-Man.
Oh, you should have been here before the Dream
When there were breasts everywhere
And the Rifle Club Parade was all
Tulips...

Future Poem

way beyond the fire-broken barricades of cars

there's the gold green blue white landscape
   of the dawn
   of the first day
   of the revolution

and i hear your gentling gentling voice
for whose gold green blue white sake
i love the revolution

Byron Is One of the Dancers

His poems – they were glad with jokes, trumpets, arguments and flying crockery
     Rejoice
He shook hearts with his lust and nonsense, he was independent as the weather
     Rejoice
Alive, alive, fully as alive as us, he used his life and let life use him
     Rejoice
He loved freedom, he loved Greece, and yes of course, he died for the freedom
  of Greece
     Rejoice

      And yes, this is a dance,
      and yes, beyond the glum farrago
      of TV cops after TV crooks
      in the blockheaded prison of TV –

      I hear the naked feet of Byron
      which skated once, powered by fascination
      over the cheerful skin of women's legs,
      I hear those two bare feet –
      One delicate and one shaped horribly –
      slap and thud, slap, thud, slap, thud,
      across the cracked-up earth of Greece,
      and yes, I hear the music which drives those feet
      and feel the arm of Byron round my shoulder
      or maybe it is round your shoulder

Oh I feel your arm around my shoulder
and yes, I know the line of dancers
across the cracked-up earth of Greece
stretches from sea to sea
as the shrivelled mountains erupt into music
and Byron and all the million dancers
yes brothers and sisters, lovers and lovers,
some lucky in life and delicately-skinned,
some shaped horribly by want or torture,
dance out the dance which must be danced

for the freedom of Greece
for the freedom of Greece

Dance
Rejoice
Dance
Rejoice

Historical Poem

The first rocket to land on Mars
Was eaten

One Question About Amsterdam

Of course it all looked good in the good light.
(Even the grandmother prostitute
Who leaned too far over her window-sill
As she picked her nose and ate it
And only stopped, with the guiltiest
Guilty start I've ever seen,
When she saw I was looking.)
Of course it all looked good,
But, since I was suspicious even in the womb,
And, as it turns out, rightly suspicious,
Forgive me, Hans, one miniature complaint.

I didn't see a single Eskimo in Amsterdam.
Everything else, yes, but no Eskimos.
Not one candle-chewing, wife-lending,
Blubber-loving igloo freak
Of an ice-hole fishing, polar bear-clobbering Nanook.
Throughout the tranquillising waterways,
Throughout the bumping wet of the harbour –
Not one bloody kayak.

Where are the eskimos of Amsterdam?
Where are the eskimos of Amsterdam?
Where are the eskimos of Amsterdam?

To the Silent Majority

ashamed to be white,
ashamed not to be in jail,
why do i keep howling about:

sky overcast with the colour of hunger,
liars who kiss like arsenic sandpaper,
white power gas, the torture game
and the one-eyed glare of that final global flame?

because they are here.

Sex Maniac Him Good

(FROM *The Second Mrs Tanqueray*)

We done it with pictures we done it with words
pounds and dollars and all
With hoare-belisha beacons and thunderbirds
at the money-fuckers' ball

Grabbed 'em by the scruff of the groin
pounds and dollars and all
Pumped 'em full of the slippery coin
at the money-fuckers' ball

Fifteen suicides screwing all night
pounds and dollars and all
Rolled in a ball down a mountain of shite
at the money-fuckers' ball

Money money money money come in a shower
pounds and dollars and all
Give me a stand like the Post Office Tower
at the money-fuckers' ball

Fucked the Bank of England and caught the pox
pounds and dollars and all
Jumped the Atlantic and buggered Fort Knox
at the money-fuckers' ball

One blind bankrupt couldn't get a screw
pounds and dollars and all
Tossed himself off with an IOU
at the money-fuckers' ball

Flag Day – But Not for the Revolution

Hunger scrapes the inside out of the human belly
Your charity small change clanks into the tin
And makes no real change.
They are not slot machines for your spare pennies
Although you can read your own gross weight
Scrawled across their faces.
The razors of hunger slash and slash and slash their skin
And all your fat pity helps no one but yourself.

276

The Dichotomy Between the Collapse
of Civilisation and Making Money
(to my students at Dartington)

No such thing as Western
civilisation
No such thing as Eastern
civilisation
The brand name for a tribe of killer apes
is civilisation

The killer apes do some little good things
So let's all do the little good things
good things good and not many of them –
Coconuts in the pacific ocean
of bad things bad things calling themselves
civilisation

What the hell if the tribe collapses
Look out look out for another tribe
of apes who do no killing but do big good things

Meanwhile look up
up above your head
only the rain is collapsing on you

Of course there's not much bread
in doing little good things
but do do do
altogether all the do do day

Because, speaking as a brother-speck
among the galaxies,
Little is the biggest we can call ourselves

Night Lines in a Peaceful Farmhouse

truth is
exactly the same size as the universe
and my eyes are narrow
i stare at one of my fingernails
its mass is pink
its edge is blue with coke-dust
it grows on a warm well-nourished hand

i look up and suck smoke
the windows are black

people are being killed

the first time I met a girl called Helen
she told me
'money is the basis of life'
the second time i met her she said
'money is the basis of life'

people are being killed

i stare at those four words
typed in black
they are true words
but they do not bleed
and die and rot

commonplace cruelty
timetable cruelty

i haven't seen much of the world
but i've seen enough

i have known more horror in half an hour
than i shall ever have the skill to tell

my right hand soothes my left hand

i have known more beauty in half a minute
than i shall ever have the skill to tell

i make a fond small smile
remembering gentleness in many cities

so many good people

and people are being killed

Display Advert

Your Strength
Your Skill
Your Gentleness
Your Imagination
Your Work
Your Beauty

the revolution needs

you

How to Kill Cuba

You must burn the people first,
Then the grass and trees, then the stones.
You must cut the island out of all the maps,
The history books, out of the old newspapers,
Even the newspapers which hated Cuba,
And burn all these, and burn
The paintings, poems and photographs and films
And when you have burnt all these
You must bury the ashes
You must guard the grave
And even then
Cuba will only be dead like Che Guevara –
Technically dead, that's all,
Technically dead.

Autobahnmotorwayautoroute

Around the gleaming map of Europe
A gigantic wedding ring
Slowly revolves through Londonoslowestberlin
Athensromemadridparis and home again,
Slowly revolving.
That's no ring,
It's the Great European Limousine,
The Famous Goldenwhite Circular Car

Slowly revolving

All the cars in Europe have been welded together
Into a mortal unity,
A roundaboutgrandtourroundabout
Trafficjamroundaboutagain,
All the cars melted together,
Citroenjaguarbugattivolkswagenporschedaf.

Each passenger, lugging his
Colourpiano, frozenmagazines, high-fidog,
Clambers over the seat in front of him
Towards what looks like the front of the car.
They are dragging behind them
Worksofart, lampshades made of human money,
Instant children and exploding clocks.

But the car's a circle
No front no back
No driver no steering wheel no windscreen no brakes no

Family Planning

Why do the Spanish have so many children?

Our first child was a priest.
Then we had a nun.
The next three were all policemen.

You've got to have one child you can talk to.

280

Open Day at Porton

These bottles are being filled with madness,
A kind of liquid madness concentrate
Which can be drooled across the land
Leaving behind a shuddering human highway...

   A welder trying to eat his arm.

   Children pushing stale food into their eyes
   To try to stop the chemical spectaculars
   Pulsating inside their hardening skulls.

   A health visitor throwing herself downstairs,
   Climbing the stairs, throwing herself down again
   Shouting: Take the nails out of my head.

There is no damage to property.

Now, nobody likes manufacturing madness,
But if we didn't make madness in bottles
We wouldn't know how to deal with bottled madness.

We don't know how to deal with bottled madness.

We all really hate manufacturing madness
But if we didn't make madness in bottles
We wouldn't know how to be sane.

Responsible madness experts assure us
Britain would never be the first
To uncork such a global brainquake.

But suppose some foreign nut sprayed Kent
With his insanity aerosol...
Well, there's only one answer to madness.

Gossip Column

Mrs Sinjohn Smackers down on the beauty farm on a diet of peasant juice and dungeon sweepings feels a small, star-shaped pain in her palatial stomach as she worries whether god is dead.

Horace Grindmate contemplates whether his mortgaged artistic talent can better be served by an advertising campaign for gold-plated broad beans or by a magazine devoted to the pornography of rolls-royce engines.

Sir Thomas Margarine, as he invents Follicle Gas, which turns hair into snakes, considers an indiscretion with both his laboratory assistants.

Somewhere in South America, an old woman gives five onions to a quiet man with a knapsack who smells of two months in the mountains.

G.I. Joe

Have you heard the big news on TV?
Have you heard the big news on TV?
On the land
In the air
On the sea
Have you heard the big news on TV?

Halt, who goes there?
G.I. Joe! Who?
G.I. Joe, that's who!
G.I. Joe! G.I. Joe!

He's the password to a merry Christmas because he's the toy soldier
Santa Claus will put beneath your Christmas tree if you tell
your folks about him. They'll enjoy watching you play with your
G.I. Joe too!

Join the fun with G.I. Joe
G.I. Joe G.I. Joe
Fighting man from head to toe
G.I. Joe G.I. Joe

Halt, who goes there?

Everybody's dream come true
G.I. Joe G.I. Joe
Looks alive and acts alive
Almost eleven inches tall
21 movable parts
G.I. Joe G.I. Joe

Run
Walk
Climb
Crawl
Throw grenades

He's tremendous

G.I. Joe G.I. Joe
G.I. Joe G.I. Joe

Uniforms for every service
All he needs for every action
Rifles
Machine guns
Flame throwers
Sandbags
Tents
Communication gear
Scuba suits
G.I. Joe G.I. Joe

From coast to coast boys are joining the G.I. Joe Club and
becoming official collectors of G.I. Joes and equipment.

Have you heard the big news on TV?
Have you heard communications gear?
Have you been eleven inches all?
Have you joined the sandbags on TV?
Fun grenade fun grenade
Fun flame fun gun
21 movable heads
Have you been eleven rifles tall?

Flame thrower from head to toe
G.I. Joe G.I. Joe
Join the flame with G.I. Joe
G.I. Joe G.I. Joe
From coast to coast
Boys are joining
Boys are running
Boys are climbing
Boys are crawling

From flame to flame
Santa's throwing
Rifle trees
Christmas guns
Christmas dreams
Christmas flames
scuba suits scuba suits scuba suits scuba suits
Join the fun join the fun
TV run
TV crawl
Dreams eleven inches tall
Flames eleven inches tall
On the land
In the air
On the sea
Flames eleven inches tall
Head to toe head to toe
Flame dreams flame dreams
Dream alive and flame alive
G.I. Joe G.I. Joe
G.I. Joe G.I. Joe
Everybody's dream come true...

Halt, who goes there?

Norman Morrison

On November 2nd 1965
in the multi-coloured multi-minded
United beautiful States of terrible America
Norman Morrison set himself on fire
outside the Pentagon.
He was thirty-one, he was a Quaker,
and his wife (seen weeping in the newsreels)
and his three children
survive him as best they can.
He did it in Washington where everyone could see
because
people were being set on fire
in the dark corners of Vietnam where nobody could see.
Their names, ages, beliefs and loves
are not recorded.
This is what Norman Morrison did.
He poured petrol over himself.
He burned. He suffered.
He died.
That is what he did
in the heart of Washington
where everyone could see.
He simply burned away his clothes,
his passport, his pink-tinted skin,
put on a new skin of flame
and became
Vietnamese.

Would You Mind Signing This Receipt?

When you get back home
You will find a black patch on the ground,
A patch of blackness shaped like a house
Where your house used to stand.

It was a mistake.
It was the wrong house.
It was all a mistake
Based on faulty information.

When you get back home
You will find three black heaps on the ground.
Three black heaps shaped like children
On the patch of blackness shaped like a house
Where your house used to stand.

It was a mistake.
They were the wrong people.
It was all a mistake
Based on faulty information.

Three children.
51 dollars compensation per child.
That comes to 153 dollars, madam.

For Rachel: Christmas 1965

Caesar sleeping in his armoured city
Herod shaking like a clockwork toy
and spies are moving into Rama
asking for a baby boy.

    Caesar is the father of Herod
    Herod is the father of us all
    and we'll be obedient, silent little children
    or the moon will drop
    and the sun will fall.

Someone must have warned the wanted mother
she'll be hiding with her family
and soldiers are marching through Rama
silently, obediently.

    Caesar is the father of Herod
    Herod is the father of us all
    and we'll be obedient, silent little children
    or the moon will drop
    and the sun will fall.

Down all the white-washed alleys of Rama
small soft bodies are bayoneted
and Rachel is weeping in Rama
and will not be comforted.

    Caesar is the father of Herod
    Herod is the father of us all
    and we'll be obedient, silent little children
    or the moon will drop
    and the sun will fall.

Caesar sleeping in his armoured city
Herod dreaming in his swansdown bed
and Rachel is weeping in Rama
and will not be comforted.

    Caesar is the father of Herod
    Herod is the father of us all
    and we'll be obedient, silent little children
    or the moon will drop
    and the sun will fall.

Thinks: I'll Finish These Gooks by Building an Electronically Operated Physical Barrier Right Along Their Seventeenth Parallel!!!

(for John Arden and Margaretta D'Arcy)

1. Thousands of miles of invisible fencing
   Distinguishable only by the balding badness of the earth
   And a slight electric shimmer in the air.

   But if you throw raw hamburger towards the sky
   It comes down grilled.

2. The Marine shouted:
   'I don't mind fighting Charlie,
   But not with my back to a goddam
   Electronically operated physical barrier.'

3. We have stopped lifting our electronic barrier
   For one hour daily at Checkpoint Harold.
   We don't mind the refugee double-deckers heading north,
   But sod this constant rumbling southwards
   Of enormous invisible wooden horses.

4. If the barrier fails
   We are going to bring in volcanoes.

5. 'I just pissed against that
   Electronically operated physical barrier,'
   Boasted the police dog to his bitch,
   'And eighty-two square miles got devastated.'

6. Tom Sawyer drew a line in the dust with his toe:
   'Step over that and I'll burn your skin off.'

7. What we really need
   Is an electronically operated physical barrier
   Around the United States.

To a Russian Soldier in Prague

You are going to be hated by the people.

They will hate you over their freakish breakfast of tripe soup and pastries.
They will squint hatred at you on their way to pretend to work.
By the light of yellow beer they will hate you with jokes you'll never hear.

You're beginning to feel
Like a landlord in a slum
Like a white man in Harlem
Like a U.S. Marine in Saigon

Socialists are hated
By all who kill for profit and power.
But you are going to be hated by
The people – who are all different.
The people – who are all extraordinary.
The people – who are all of equal value.
Socialism is theirs, it was invented for them.
Socialism is theirs, it can only be made by them.

Africa, Asia and Latin America are screaming:
STARVATION. POVERTY. OPPRESSION.
When they turn to America.
They see only flames and children in the flames.
When they turn to England
They see an old lady in a golden wheelchair,
Share certificates in one hand, a pistol in the other.
When they turn to Russia
They see – you.

You are going to be hated
As the English have usually been hated.
The starving, the poor and the oppressed
Are turning, turning away.
While you nervously guard a heap of documents
They stagger away through the global crossfire
Towards revolution, towards socialism.

From the Statement of a Vietnamese Buddhist Monk

The secret police came to me in the middle of the night
and said: 'Do you believe in God?'

Goodbye Richard Nixon

Your California bedroom was red white and blue
You won ten thousand dollars playing poker in the Navy
Your College football team was called The Poets
And you tucked the bottom of your tie into the top of your trousers
    Gave you a sort of safe feeling

You had a music box played Hail to the Chief
Your favourite building was the Lincoln Memorial
Your favourite food was cottage cheese and ketchup
Your favourite Xmas song was Rudolph the Red-Nosed Reindeer
    And you never wiped your arse

Ceasefire
(dedicated to the Medical Aid Committee for Vietnam)

The outside of my body was half-eaten
by fire which clings as tight as skin.
The fire has turned some of my skin
into black scab bits of roughness
and some pale bits smooth as plastic,
which no one dares touch
except me and the doctor.
Everyone who looks at me is scared.
That's not because I want to hurt people
but because so much of me
looks like the meat of a monster...

I was walking to the market.
Then I was screaming.
They found me screaming.
They put out the flames on my skin.
They laid me on a stretcher and I cried:
Not on my back!
So they turned me over and I cried:
Not on my front!

A doctor put a needle in my arm
and my mind melted
and I fell into a furnace of dreams of furnaces.

When I woke up I was in a white hospital.
Everything I wanted to say scared me
and I did not want to scare the others
in that white hospital,
so I said nothing, cried as quietly as I could.

Months passed over my head
and bombers passed over my head
and people came and said they were my parents
and they found out the places on my face
where I could bear to be kissed.

And I pretended I could see them
but I couldn't really look out of my eyes
but only inwards, into my head
where the flames still clung and hurt, and talked.

And the flames said:
You are meat.
You are ugly meat.
Your body cannot grow to loveliness.
Nobody could love such ugly meat.
Only ugly meat could love such ugly meat.
Better be stewed for soup and eaten.

And months passed over my head
and bombers passed over my head
and the voices of the flames began to flicker
and I began to believe the people who said they were my parents
were my parents.

And one day I threw myself forward
so that I sat up in bed, for the first time,
and hurled my arms around my mother,
and however the skin of my chest howled out in its pain
I held her, I held her, I held her
and knew she was my mother.
And I forgot that I was monster meat
and I knew she did not know that I was monster meat.

I held her, I held her.

And, sweet sun which blesses all the world –
all the flames faded.
The flames of my skin
and the flames inside my head –
all the flames faded
and I was flooded
with love for my mother
who did not know
that I was monster meat.

And so, in the love-flood, I let go of my mother
and fell back upon my pillow
and I rolled my head to the left side
and I saw a child, or it might have been an old man,
eating his rice with his only arm
and I rolled my head to the right side
and saw another child, or she might have been an old woman,
being fed through the arm from a tube from a red bottle –
and I loved them, and, flooded with love
I started to sing
the song of the game I used to play with my friends
in the long-ago days before the flames came:

    One, one, bounce the ball,
    Once for the sandal-maker,
    Two, two, bounce the ball,
    Twice for the fishermen on the river.
    Three, three, bounce the ball,
    Three times for your golden lover –

And had to stop singing.
Throat choked with vomit.

And then the flames exploded again all over my skin
and then the flames exploded again inside my head
and I burned, sweet sun, sweet mother, I burned.

    Sweet sun, which blesses all the world,
    this was one of the people of Vietnam.

I suppose we love each other.
We're stupid if we don't.

We have a choice –
Either choke to death on our own vomit
or to become one
with the sweet sun, which blesses all the world.

To Whom It May Concern (Tell Me Lies about Vietnam)

I was run over by the truth one day.
Ever since the accident I've walked this way
    So stick my legs in plaster
    Tell me lies about Vietnam.

Heard the alarm clock screaming with pain,
Couldn't find myself so I went back to sleep again
    So fill my ears with silver
    Stick my legs in plaster
    Tell me lies about Vietnam.

Every time I shut my eyes all I see is flames.
Made a marble phone book and I carved all the names
    So coat my eyes with butter
    Fill my ears with silver
    Stick my legs in plaster
    Tell me lies about Vietnam.

I smell something burning, hope it's just my brains.
They're only dropping peppermints and daisy-chains
    So stuff my nose with garlic
    Coat my eyes with butter
    Fill my ears with silver
    Stick my legs in plaster
    Tell me lies about Vietnam.

Where were you at the time of the crime?
Down by the Cenotaph drinking slime
   So chain my tongue with whisky
   Stuff my nose with garlic
   Coat my eyes with butter
   Fill my ears with silver
   Stick my legs in plaster
   Tell me lies about Vietnam.

You put your bombers in, you put your conscience out,
You take the human being and you twist it all about
   So scrub my skin with women
   Chain my tongue with whisky
   Stuff my nose with garlic
   Coat my eyes with butter
   Fill my ears with silver
   Stick my legs in plaster
   Tell me lies about Vietnam.

Peace Is Milk

Peace is milk.
War is acid.
The elephant dreams of bathing in lakes of milk.
Acid blood
Beats through the veins
Of the monstrous, vulture-weight fly,
Shaking, rocking his framework.

The elephants, their gentle thinking shredded
By drugs disseminated in the electricity supply,
Sell their children, buy tickets for the Zoo
And form a dead-eyed queue
Which stretches from the decorative, spiked gates
To the enormous shed where the flies are perching.

Peace is milk
War is acid.
Sometimes an elephant finds a bucket of milk.
Swash! and it's empty.
The fly feeds continually.
The fly bulges with acid
Or he needs more. And more.

An overweight fly levers himself
From his revolving chair,
Paces across the elephantskin floor,
Presses a button
And orders steak, steak, elephant steak
And a pint of acid.

Peace is milk.
War is acid.
The elephants are being dried in the sun.
The huge flies overflow.

Look down from the plane.
Those clouds of marvellous milk.
Easily they swing by on the wind,
Assembling, disassembling,
Forming themselves into pleasure-towers,
Unicorns, waterfalls, funny faces;
Swimming, basking, dissolving –
Easily, easily.

Tomorrow the cream-clouds will be fouled.
The sky will be buckshot-full of paratroop swarms
With their money-talking guns,
Headlines carved across their foreheads,
Sophisticated, silent electrical equipment.
Heart-screws and fear-throwers.
The day after tomorrow
The clouds will curdle, the clouds will begin to burn –
Yes, we expected that, knew about that,
Overkill, overburn, multi-megacorpse,
Yeah, yeah, yeah we knew about that
Cry the white-hearted flies.

Channel One –
A fly scientist in an ivory helmet
Who always appears about to cry
Explains why the viewers have to die.

Channel Nine –
A fly statesman,
Hardly audible through the acid rain,
Explains why nothing can ever happen again.

Oh we'll soon be finished with the creatures of the earth.
There's no future in elephants, milk or Asiatics.

We should be working out
How to inflict the maximum pain
On Martians and Venusians.

Sour sky.
The elephants are entering the shed.
Sour sky.
The flies have dropped a star called Wormwood
And turned the Pacific into an acid bath.
Sour sky.
Socrates said no harm could come to a good man,
But even Socrates
Couldn't turn the hemlock into a banana milk shake
With one high-voltage charge
From his Greek-sky eyes.
Even Socrates, poor bugger.

They are rubbing their forelegs together,
Washing each others' holes with their stubbled tongues,
Watching us while they wash.

Then, like brown rain running backwards,
They hurtle upwards, vibrating with acid.
They patrol our ceilings, always looking downwards.
Pick up the phone, that's them buzzing.
The turd-born flies.

Peace is milk
And milk is simple
And milk is hard to make.
It takes clean grass, fed by clean earth, clear air, clean rain,
Takes a calm cow with all her stomachs working
And it takes milk to raise that cow.

The milk is not for the good elephant.
The milk is not for the bad elephant.
But the milk may be for the lucky elephant
Looming along until the end of the kingdom of the flies.

A family of people, trapped in Death Valley,
Drank from the radiator,
Laid out the hubcaps as bowls for the dew,
Buried each other up to the neck in sand
And waited for better times, which came
Just after they stopped hoping.

So the sweet survival of the elephants demands
Vision, cunning, energy and possibly burial
Until, maybe, the good times roll for the first time
And a tidal wave of elephants,
A stampede of milk,
Tornadoes through the capitals of flydom,
Voices flow like milk,
And below the white, nourishing depths –
Bodies moving any way they want to move,
Eyes resting or dancing at will,
Limbs and minds which follow, gladly,
The music of the milk.

So you drink my milk, I'll drink yours.
We'll melt together in the sun
Despite the high-explosive flies
Which hover, which hover,
Which hover, which hover,
Like a million plaguey Jehovahs.

Their prisons, their police, their armies, their laws,
Their camps where Dobermans pace the cadaver of a field,
Their flame factories and Black Death Factories,
The sourness of their sky –
Well that's the poisonous weather the elephants must lumber through
Surviving, surviving,
Until the good times roll for the first time.

But it doesn't end
With an impregnable city carved out of the living light.
It doesn't end
In the plastic arms of an Everest-size Sophia Loren.
It doesn't end
When the world says a relieved farewell to the white man
As he goofs off to colonise the Milky Way.

It continues, it continues.
When all of the elephants push it goes slowly forward.
When they stop pushing it rolls backwards.
It continues, it continues.
Towards milk, towards acid.

The taste of milk has been forgotten.
Most elephants agree peace is impossible.
Choosing death instead, they are jerked towards death
Slowly by newspapers, nightmares or cancer,
More quickly by heroin or war.

And some, the tops of their skulls sliced off
By money-knives or the axes of guilt,
Bow their great heads and let their hurting brains
Slop in the lavatory to drown.

There are prophets like Ginsberg – grandson of William Blake –
Desperate elephants who drink a pint of diamonds.
Their eyes become scored with a thousand white trenches,
Their hide shines with a constellation
Of diamond-headed boils,
Each footstep leaves a pool of diamond dust.
And sure, they shine,
They become shouting stars,
Burning with light until they are changed by pain
Into diamonds for everyone.
And sure, they go down shining,
They shine themselves to death,
The diamond drinkers.

The world is falling to pieces
But some of the pieces taste good.

There are various ways of making peace,
Most of them too childish for English elephants.
Given time and love it's possible
To cultivate a peace-field large enough
For the playing of a child.
It's possible to prepare a meal
And give it with care and love
To someone who takes it with care and love.
These are beginnings, but it's late, late –
TV Dinner tonight.
It's possible to suck the taste of peace
From one blade of grass
Or recognise peace in a can of white paint,
But it's not enough.
In Nirvana there's only room for one at a time.

WELL, YOU COULD STOP KILLING PEOPLE FOR A START,

Let loose the elephants.
Let the fountains talk milk.
Free the grass, let it walk wherever it likes.
Let the passports and prisons burn, their smoke turning into milk.
Let the pot-smokers blossom into milk-coloured mental petals.
We all need to be breast-fed
And start again.

Tear the fly-woven lying suits
Off the backs of the white killers
And let their milky bodies
Make naked pilgrimage
To wash the sores of Africa and Asia
With milk, for milk is peace
And money tastes of guns,
Guns taste of acid.

Make love well, generously, deeply.
There's nothing simpler in the savage world,
Making good love, making good good love.
There's nothing harder in the tender world,
Making good love, making good good love,
And most of the elephants, most of the time
Go starving for good love, not knowing what the pain is,
But it can be done and thank Blake it is done,
Making good love, making good good love.
In houses built of fly turds, in fly-turd feasting mansions,
Fly fear insurance offices even,
Fly-worshipping cathedrals even,
Even in murder offices just off the corridors of fly power –
Making good love, making good good love.

Good lovers float.
Happy to know they are becoming real.
They float out above the sourness, high on the seeds of peace.
There are too few of them up there.
Too little milk.
Drink more milk.
Breed more cows and elephants.
Think more milk and follow your banana.
We need evangelist, door-to-door lovers,
Handing it out, laying it down,
Spreading the elephant seed, delivering the revolutionary milk,
Making good love, making good good love.
United Nations teams of roving elephant milkmen
Making good love, making good good love,
Because peace is milk,
Peace is milk
And the skinny, thirsty earth, its face covered with flies,
Screams like a baby.

A Tourist Guide to England

£ Welcome to England!
England is a happy country

£ Here is a happy English businessman.
Hating his money, he spends it all
On bibles for Cambodia
And a charity to preserve
The Indian Cobra from extinction.

£ I'm sorry you can't see our happy coal-miners.
Listen hard and you can hear them
Singing Welsh hymns far underground.
Oh. The singing seems to have stopped.

£ No, that is not Saint Francis of Assisi.
That is a happy English policeman.

£ Here is a happy black man.
No, it is not illegal to be black. Not yet.

£ Here are the slums.
They are preserved as a tourist attraction.
Here is a happy slum-dweller.
Hello, slum-dweller!
No, his answer is impossible to translate.

£ Here are some happy English schoolchildren.
See John. See Susan. See Mike.
They are studying for their examinations.
Study, children, study!
John will get his O-Levels
And an O-Level job and an O-Level house and an O-Level wife.
Susan will get her A-Levels
And an A-Level job and an A-Level house and an A-Level husband.
Mike will fail.

£ Here are some happy English soldiers.
They are going to make the Irish happy.

£ No, please understand.
We understand the Irish
Because we've been sending soldiers to Ireland
For hundreds and hundreds of years.

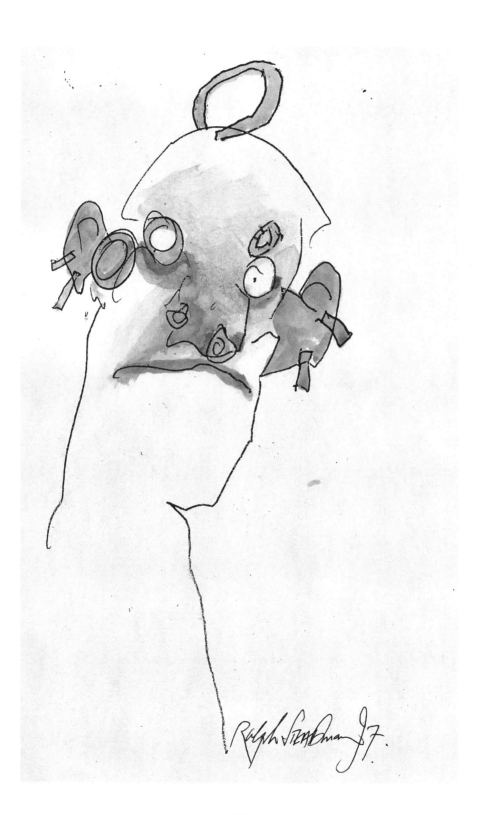

£ First we tried to educate them
   With religion, famine and swords.
   But the Irish were slow to learn.

£ So now we are trying to educate them
   With truncheons, gas, rubber bullets,
   Steel bullets, internment and torture,
   We are trying to teach the Irish
   To be as happy as us.

£ So please understand us
   And if your country
   Should be forced to educate
   Another country in the same way,
   Or your own citizens in the same way –
   We will try to understand you.

Ode to the Sponsors of the British Appeal
Committee of Europalia '73
(*or:* Who's Who in International Daylight Robbery)

O Lord Adeane, Lord Aldington
Sir Cyril Kleinwort, Kleinwort Benson,
        Intercede for us.
O ICI, O Rio Tinto Zinc
        Colonise us in our unworthiness.
O Sir Paul Chambers, KBE,
        In our hour of need.
O Rothschild and Sons, Phoenix Assurance,
Sir Martin Wilkinson, The Stock Exchange,
The Honourable Sir Marcus Sieff of Marks and Spencer
        Shower thy blessings.
O Maxwell Joseph, Walney Mann
British American Tobacco Co.
        Deliver us from cancer.
O Sotheby's, EMI, Metal Box Company,
        Do what thou will with us,
O General Fire and Life Assurance,
        Reassure and interfere with us.
O Whitbreads, Sidney Spiro, Slough Estates,
        Won't you slip it to us?

O Hon John Baring, Baring Foundation,
Instone Bloomfield of Oddeninos,
      Really do it to us.
O British Petroleum, O Guinness, Bank of England,
      Come on, won't you sock it to us?
O Viscount Harcourt, O Sir Eric Jack Lyons,
Colonel J.D. Fitzjohn, Sir Eric Roll, Lord Goodman
And others too powerful to mention –
      I mean, really stick it up us.
Sir Don Ryder, ride us.
Sir Max Rayne, rain upon us.
Sir Brian Mountain, mount upon us –

      I see your names
      Written in flames.

Sorry Bout That

Truth is a diamond
A diamond is hard
You don't exist
Without a Barclaycard

Sorry bout that
Sorry bout that
Even South African cops
Do the sorry bout that

They showed me the world and said:
What do you think?
I said: half about women
And half about drink

And I'm sorry bout that
Sorry bout that
Mother, I need that booze
And I'm sorry bout that

If you cut your conscience
Into Kennomeat chunks
You can get elected
To the House of Drunks

Sorry bout that
Sorry bout that
You'll never have to think again
And I'm sorry bout that

You can do the Skull
Or the Diplomat
But I do a dance called
The Sorry Bout That

Do the Mighty Whitey
Or the Landlord Rat
But I'll keep grooving to
The Sorry Bout That

Sorry bout that
Sorry bout that
They make me dance with pistols and ten to one
I'm sorry bout that

I saw Money walking
Down the road
Claws like an eagle
And a face like a toad

Well I know your name baby
Seen you before
Slapping on your make-up
For the Third World War

Sorry bout that
Sorry bout that
Someone set the world on fire
And I'm sorry bout that

Victor Jara of Chile

(This ballad has been set to music and recorded by Arlo Guthrie)

Victor Jara of Chile
Lived like a shooting star
He fought for the people of Chile
With his songs and his guitar

And his hands were gentle
His hands were strong

Victor Jara was a peasant
Worked from a few years old
He sat upon his father's plough
And watched the earth unfold

And his hands were gentle
His hands were strong

When the neighbours had a wedding
Or one of their children died
His mother sang all night for them
With Victor by her side

And his hands were gentle
His hands were strong

He grew to be fighter
Against the people's wrongs
He listened to their grief and joy
And turned them into songs

And his hands were gentle
His hands were strong

He sang about the copper miners
And those who work the land
He sang about the factory workers
And they knew he was their man

And his hands were gentle
His hands were strong

He campaigned for Allende
Working night and day
He sang: take hold of your brother's hand
The future begins today

And his hands were gentle
His hands were strong

The bloody generals seized Chile
They arrested Victor then
They caged him in a stadium
With five thousand frightened men

And his hands were gentle
His hands were strong

Victor stood in the stadium
His voice was brave and strong
He sang for his fellow-prisoners
Till the guards cut short his song

And his hands were gentle
His hands were strong

They broke the bones in both his hands
They beat his lovely head
They tore him with electric shocks
After two long days of torture they shot him dead

And his hands were gentle
His hands were strong

And now the Generals rule Chile
And the British have their thanks
For they rule with Hawker Hunters
And they rule with Chieftain tanks

And his hands were gentle
His hands were strong

Victor Jara of Chile
Lived like a shooting star
He fought for the people of Chile
With his songs and his guitar

And his hands were gentle
His hands were strong

Astrid-Anna

*(This piece was written especially for an Anglo-German audience
at the Goethe Institute in London)*

Here is a news item from a right-wing British paper – the *Daily Mail.*

TERROR GIRL IS ILL
'Baader Meinhof girl Astrid Proll, who faces extradition to Germany, is physic-
ally and mentally ill, her friends said yesterday. They gathered outside Bow
Street magistrates court...and handed out leaflets saying she was having diffi-
culty in breathing and had "sensations of panic". Carnations were thrown to
her as she was led away.'

If Astrid Proll, who is now a British citizen by marriage – Anna Puttick – is
sent back to Germany, she will be dead within two years. There are special
sections in special prisons in Germany where prisoners like Astrid-Anna find
it easy to obtain revolvers. Even odder, they do not shoot their jailers. They
shoot out their own brains. If the British hand over Astrid-Anna to the West
German police, we will be collaborating in yet another murder. Well, we done
a few before.

> Sensations of panic
> Carnations were thrown
> Free Astrid   Free Anna

Astrid-Anna was accused of the attempted murder of two policemen.
But she has never been found guilty of anything.
But she was the first prisoner in Germany to be kept in conditions of SENSORY
DEPRIVATION. In the Silent Wing of the Women's Psychiatric Unit at Ossen-
dorf Prison in Cologne.

There are white walls, constant lighting, no external sounds – techniques
designed to disorientate and subdue. She spent a total of FOUR AND A HALF
MONTHS in the Silent Wing. About TWENTY-FOUR WEEKS in the Silent
Wing. About ONE THOUSAND SEVEN HUNDRED HOURS in the Silent
Wing.

Her trial was stopped by a doctor. He found the following complaints: weakness
and exhaustion, the feeling of 'being wrapped in cotton wool', dizziness, black-
outs, headaches and no appetite, feelings of breaking down, an inability to
concentrate, increasing signs of phobia and agoraphobia. Her blood circulation
began to collapse, depriving her brain of oxygen. Continued imprisonment,
said the doctor, would lead to PERMANENT AND IRREPARABLE DAMAGE.

Four and a half months
In the silent wing
Four and a half months
in the silent wing

Shut in a white box
Under the constant neon
Being whitened in a box
Under the silent neon
Boxed in the white neon
Of the silent box
Under the constant wing.

In the white of the silent box
In the silence of the white box
In the constant silence
In the constant white
In the white of the white box

    Your head starts exploding
    Your skull is about to split
    Your spine is drilling into your brain
    You are pissing your brains away

In the white of the silent box
In the silence of the white box
In the constant silence
In the constant white
In the white of the white box

    Under the Nazis an experiment was made in which they locked a man
    in a white cell with white furniture. He wore white clothes. And all
    his food and drink were white. He very soon lost his appetite. He
    could not eat. He could not drink. The sight of the white food and
    the white drink made him vomit.

Astrid came to England and began life again as Anna. She worked with young
people in the East End as an instructor in car mechanics. One Englishwoman
says: 'Anna gave me and my children enormous support...When I was drink-
ing too much, it was Anna who cared enough to see why and then helped me
to make decisions that I was drinking to forget.'

    This is the Terror Girl of the *Daily Mail*.

Now Anna is being kept under maximum-security conditions in a man's prison
– Brixton. There are only two women in the prison. They are supervised by

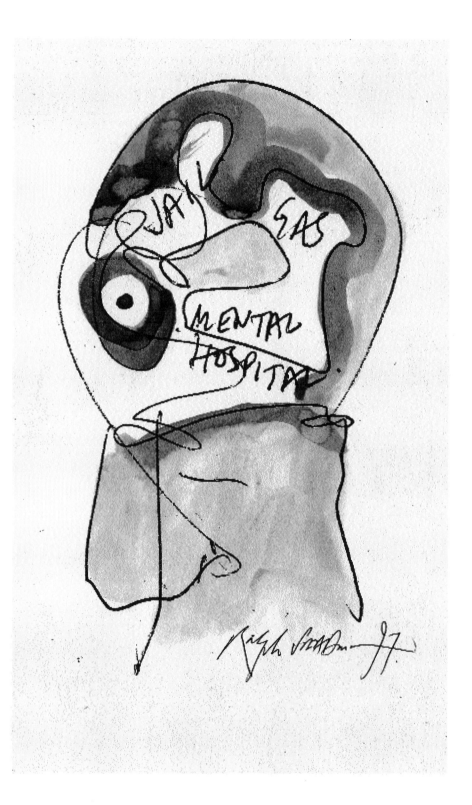

309

seven warders. They have no privacy. When Anna has a visitor, her conversation is listened to. When her lawyer visits her in her cell below the court, there is always a policeman in the cell. For three hours a day she is allowed to meet the other woman in Brixton jail. The rest of the time she spends on her own.

> So will Anna be sent back by our rulers
> to the white of the white box
> to the silence of the white silence
> to the constant silence and the constant white
> to the whiteness of the silence
> to the silence of the whiteness
> to the whiteness of the whiteness
> to the silence of the silence
> to the whiteness of the whiteness
> to the silence of the silence
> to the whiteness to the silence to the whiteness to the silence
> whiteness   whiteness   silence   silence

Stop. You can stop them. If Anna is extradited or not depends on the Home Secretary. Write to the Home Secretary. Demand she be allowed to stay. Demand that she be treated humanely. And if you are German, force your government to be satisfied with its revenge, to drop its demands for extradition, to drop the case against her, to close the Silent Wing forever.

> We will walk out from here
> into the blue-eyed, brown-faced, green-haired world
> our spinning, singing planet
> but Anna who was Astrid lies chained in the box of the state
> silent men in suits walk towards her with blank faces
> they carry syringes and hooks and guns in their white briefcases

LET ANNA STAY HERE
LET HER WORK
LET HER REST
LET HER FIND LOVE

The Airline Steward's Spiel

Oxygen masks
Four at each side
Whenever you see one
You need one
So grab one

I've never
Seen them come down
And my wife and I
Would like to keep it that way

Have a pleasant flight

Activities of an East and West Dissident Blues

(verses to be read by the Secret Police, the chorus to be read by anyone else)

When I woke up this morning it was nothing o'clock
I erased all the dreams from my head
I washed my face in shadow-juice
And for breakfast I ate my bed

I said goodbye to my jailer and spy
Burnt letters from all of my friends
Then I caught the armoured bus for a mystery tour
To the street with two dead ends

and oh
I wish I had a great big shiny brass diver's helmet
and I wish I had great big leaden diver's boots on me
and I wish I had infallible mates upstairs at the air-pumps
as I wandered forever on the bottom of the great free sea

I arrived at my factory or office or field
I did what I was meant to do
I left undone what should be left undone
And all of the others did the same thing too
      And you too? Right.

311

In the evening I read whatever should be read
Listened to whatever should be heard
And I taught the top twenty government slogans
To my golden-caged security bird

And I changed into the pair of pyjamas
With a number stamped on brown and black bars
And I pulled down the blind to keep out of my mind
The excitement of the stars

but oh
I wish I had a great big shining brass diver's helmet
and I wish I had great big leaden diver's boots on me
and infallible mates upstairs with their hands on the air-pumps
as I wandered forever on the bottom of the great green
flowing free and easy sea

24 Orders with (Optional) Adjectives

fetch my (happy) screwdriver
smell those (sugary) goldfish
shut that (amazing) door
touch my (scrawny) statues
close your (intricate) eyes
fill up the (Russian) hole again
tell your (gaping) sister
put that (shining) bomb together
spare my (murky) child
show your (grey) feelings
put up your (smiling) hand
hide your (iron) face
hand over those (solemn) emeralds
don't try to get (red-handled) funny with me
wash their (impertinent) car
cut its (sweet) throat
eat your (exclusive) cabbage
take down your (little) trousers
make up your (agile) mind
get down on your (frightening) knees
stick to your own (pathetic) kind
take the (stupid) tea
polish those (harmonious) boots

Carol During the Falklands Experience

In the blind midslaughter
The drowned sank alone
Junta set like concrete
Thatcher like a stone

Blood had fallen, blood on blood,
Blood on blood
In the blind midslaughter
In the madness flood

What shall I give them
Powerless as I am?
If I were a rich man
I wouldn't give a damn

If I were an arms dealer
I would play my part –
All I can do is point towards
The holy human heart.

The Reindeer Rider in an Old Russian Photograph

The reindeer rider could only speak
A Russian brand of Turkish
While the best that I can manage
Is a sort of British English.
Besides the reindeer rider died
In the last century
While I'm in the top front left-hand seat
Of a double-decker called Mortuáry.
But seeing him on that reindeer's back
I want to warn him to pin his ears back,
For, while he seems to think: so far so good,
That reindeer is obviously a no-good
And its eye is full of mischief
As an oak is full of oak-wood.

Chile in Chains

'Student demonstrators yesterday forced the Chilean Ambassador to clamber over rooftops and hide in a kitchen after they broke up a meeting he was trying to address at St John's College, Cambridge. The Ambassador, Professor Miguel Schweitzer, was invited to talk to the Monday Club on diplomatic relations between Britain and Chile...' *The Guardian*, 13 November 1980.

'Any victory for the people, however small, is worth celebrating' – a demonstrator.

'I've never seen an Ambassador running before, so I'm not quite sure how to rate him as a runner' – a Cambridge spectator.

There's eight men in Cambridge called the Monday Club,
It's like the British Movement with brains,
And they thought it cute to pay a sort of tribute
To the government of Chile in Chains.

So the Mondays invited the Ambassador
To St John's as their honoured guest –
But he must come unto them secretly
(At the Special Branch's special request).

The Ambassador was glad to get an invite –
He flicked off his electric shock machine,
Scrubbed the blood from under his fingernails
And summoned his bodyguard and limousine.

'What shall I tell them?' the Ambassador mused
As he flushed his better self down the loo,
'Allende was a mass murderer
But Pinochet is Jesus Mark Two?

'What shall I tell them?' the Ambassador thought
As his car snaked down Cambridgeshire lanes,
'That Victor Jara tortured himself to death
And Paradise is Chile in Chains?'

But as they were proffering South African sherry
The faces of the Monday Club froze –
For a mob of Lefties had assembled outside:
Socialist and Anarchist desperadoes!

So they switched their venue from the Wordsworth Room
To the Wilberforce Room, locked the doors
And the Monday Club gave its limp applause
To a pimp for fascist whores.

314

But the revolution never stops
(We even go marching when it rains),
And a Yale lock is no protection at all
For a salesman for Chile in Chains.

When the Left tumbled into the Wilberforce Room
The Ambassador was terrified.
His bodyguard shovelled him out the back door
And the Monday Club was occupied.

Oh they hurried him over the rooftops
And the pigeons gave him all they had.
Oh they hid him away in the kitchen
And all of the food went bad.

But the Left sat down in the Wilberforce Room.
The atmosphere smelled of shame.
Then a Don said: 'This is private property.
Tell me your college and name.'

'We didn't come to talk about property.
We came to talk about the pains
Of the poor and the murdered and the tortured and the raped
Who are helpless in Chile in Chains.'

They grouped a scrum of cops round their honoured guest
And we jeered at him and his hosts
As he ran with the cops across the grass of the Court
Like a torturer pursued by ghosts.

He galloped with his minders to his limousine
But the stink of his terror remains
And everyone who watched his cowardly run
Knows – Chile will tear off her chains.

A Prayer for the Rulers of this World

God bless their suits
God bless their ties
God bless their grubby
Little alibis

God bless their firm,
Commanding jaws
God bless their thumbs
God bless their claws

God bless their livers
God bless their lungs
God bless their
Shit-encrusted tongues

God bless their prisons
God bless their guns
God bless their deaf and dumb
Daughters and sons

God bless their corpuscles
God bless their sperms
God bless their souls
Like little white worms

Oh God will bless
The whole bloody crew
For God, we know,
Is a ruler too

And the blessed shall live
And the damned shall die
And God will rule
In his suit and his tie

'Appendix IV

Requirements in the Shelter

  Clothing
  Cooking Equipment
  Food
  Furniture
  Hygiene
  Lighting
  Medical
  Shrouds'

What?

  'Shrouds.
  Several large, strong black plastic bags
  and a reel of 2-inch, or wider, adhesive tape
  can make adequate air-tight containers
  for deceased persons
  until the situation permits burial.'

No I will not put my lovely wife into a large strong black plastic bag
No I will not put my lovely children into large strong black plastic bags
No I will not put my lovely dog or my lovely cats into large strong black
    plastic bags
I will embrace them all until I am filled with their radiation

Then I will carry them, one by one
Through the black landscape
And lay them gently at the concrete door
Of the concrete block
Where the colonels
And the chief detectives
And the MPs
And the Regional Commissioners
Are biding their time

And then I will lie down with my wife and children
And my dog and my cats

And we will wait for the door to open

One Bad Word

(for my Black and Asian friends and their children
who are threatened in the streets)

You call me that bad word
That one bad word
That bad word weighs a thousand tonne
That one bad word burns my skin all over
You call me one bad word
That word makes my mother
Cast down her eyes in shame
Makes my father
Deny his own name
Makes my brother
Turn and fight like a demon
Makes my sister
Spend her life in bad dreaming

So call me one bad word
And you don't know what will happen
It could be tears it could be blood
I could be storm
It could be silence
It could be a rage
Hot enough to burn the whole town down
Could be a stampede of elephants
Through your back garden
And into your mother's
Frilly perfume sitting room.
Could be zombie nightmares
Every night for the rest
Of your natural life
Could be all your food
From this day on
Will taste of rotten fishheads
Could be anything
Could be the end of the world
But most likely
This will follow:

I'll stare at you
For one cold second
And then I'll turn and walk away from you
Leaving you alone with yourself
And your one bad word